Charles H. Goren's
100 Challenging
Bridge Hands
for you to enjoy

Charles H. Goren's
100 Challenging Bridge Hands
for you to enjoy

Chas H. Goren

Test your skill against the Master's winning way to play and defend

Introduction by Omar Sharif

A **CHANCELLOR HALL** *Book published by*

DOUBLEDAY & COMPANY, INC. *Garden City, N. Y.*

ACKNOWLEDGEMENTS

In addition to the valuable contributions of the Goren Editorial Board, I am indebted to Ray Brown, Fred Karpin and Thomas M. Smith for special assistance in the selection of material and checking the accuracy of this book.

Charles H. Goren

Introduction

Ever since 1931, when he first made his appearance in the world of tournament bridge, Charles Goren has been playing and writing about bridge, with such eclat that his accomplishments in both endeavors put him indisputably at the top.

In the course of his long career, one must estimate that he has played, observed or written about some half a million bridge hands. Therefore, the one hundred he has chosen to present here are, as might be expected, truly fascinating and unusual. Each deal is a gem, either because it presents a challenge or because it offers a lesson in technique — not just the technique of play or defense, but the technique of what and how to think about the problems and possible pitfalls involved.

Unless you are already a super-expert, you are about to encounter many situations you have never met before; problems that had to be solved from scratch when first they were met in actual play. You have one advantage; you know that there is a danger to be overcome or an opportunity to be found in every deal.

I promise that you will find this book much like playing in a perfect game of bridge, where only the most interesting and dramatic hands are allowed to be dealt and where you move about the table so that you occupy the decision seat on every hand. There is manna here for many fruitful sessions in which you can take as long as you want without annoying any of the other players. Enjoy. Enjoy.

Omar Sharif

CONTENTS

An Intriguing Challenge from Charles Goren

This is a different kind of bridge book for me, and I hope for you as well. It is like playing bridge with a pencil; no cards or opponents are required.

From a long career of playing bridge, watching bridge and reading bridge, I have selected one hundred challenging hands I have encountered. They are aimed at entertaining you; at testing your skill; at instructing you, not merely by showing you the best way to tackle certain bridge problems, but the right way to think about the winning answer — sometimes as a defender, more often as declarer.

These are NOT double-dummy problems. Although all four hands are shown in the diagrams, the cards you see when the challenge is set forth are printed in bold, black type. The "unseen" hands are grayed down: legible enough to let you check your solution, but faint enough so that you can avoid peeking if you want to. (In fact, if you wish to cover the grayed-down hands, you can do so very simply by using a triangle to cover declarer's and partner's hands, or a rectangular cut-out to reveal only declarer's hand and the dummy.)

The contents have been arranged to present first a group of declarer's play exercises; then defensive problems, first for East and then for West; finally a group of the more difficult hands and a couple of story-book deals.

Another innovation is the size of the diagrams and the space between each card. There is plenty of room (and the paper for this book has been selected) so you can take a pencil and circle or cross out cards as you "play" them, then erase and try again if you wish to follow another plan. Putting it another way, this has been designed as a play book, a work book and, I hope, a fun book.

However, it is NOT a book for inexperienced players. Indeed, if you are keeping score and give yourself 10 points for each correct solution, you will be doing extremely well if your total is 700 to 790; rate yourself a superior player if you score from 810 to 900; if your total is above 900, you must be an expert enjoying a pleasant exercise of skill.

No matter what your eventual total, I promise that by the time you are halfway through this book you will have added points to your score at the table and enjoyment to your game next time you play.

Charles H. Goren

September, 1976

Vulnerable: N-S
Dealer: N

```
                    ♠ Q 6 2
                    ♡ J 7
                    ♦ A J 2
                    ♣ A K 8 6 2
♠ 8 4                              ♠ K 10 9 5 3
♡ A Q 10 9 6 2        N           ♡ K
♦ 8 3             W       E        ♦ 9 7 6 5
♣ J 7 4               S           ♣ Q 5 3
                    ♠ A J 7
                    ♡ 8 5 4 3
                    ♦ K Q 10 4
                    ♣ 10 9
```

The bidding:

NORTH	EAST	SOUTH	WEST
1♣	2♠	2NT	3♡
3NT	Pass	Pass	Pass

Opening lead: ♠ 8

It is difficult to decide whether to present this deal as a problem for the declarer or for the defense. However, since the declarer made a brilliant play and I, sitting West, failed to rise to the occasion, I will give you the same chance to outwit me and let you sit South.

East, I might explain, was the late Adam Meredith, one of England's all-time greats, who often bid spades on three-card suits and saw nothing unusual about a jump bid with only five. Anyway, as South, the ♠ 8 has been passed round to your ♠ J and you can see that once you lose the lead the opponents can run the heart suit. How do you cope?

your chance to take advantage of Goren   1.

When South won the first trick with the ♠ J, he was able to count eight top tricks. But how was he to get a ninth with the heart suit ready to be run against him the moment he lost the lead? Take time out to think as South did.

It was reasonable to figure that West's heart bid at the three level was based on a six-card suit, especially as he had no support for partner's spade bid. Obviously the suit did not include the three top honors or West would have led it. And, if it was true that West held six hearts, then East must have a singleton.

Well, if West held six to the K Q 10 9, he probably would have opened a heart rather than trust one of Meredith's notoriously weird spade bids. And with six to the ♡ A K, West might have led the ♡ K to have a look around. On this reasoning, South figured that East probably had the ♡ K alone and he schemed to play so that the

defenders would cut their own communications.

He promptly cashed four diamond tricks, with West high-lowing in hearts on the last two while East followed to all four. North's discard was a low club.

Next came the Machiavellian play — a low heart toward dummy's ♡ J. Maybe I should have figured it out and gone up with the ♡ A. I know now that I should have. But, instead, I played the ♡ Q. Perforce, East had to overtake with the ♡ K. He did his best to get out of the trap by leading the ♣ Q, but declarer countered by ducking this trick. Now, although dummy's long club was established, East had to continue the club suit to avoid leading away from the ♠ K and giving declarer an overtrick.

Neither Adam nor I shone on this deal, but I am glad to have an opportunity to pay him tribute, even at the cost of exposing my feet of clay.

♠ A Q J 10
♡ A Q 5 3
◇ K J 6
♣ 4 2

	N	
♠ 8 7 6 5	W E	♠ 9 4 2
♡ J 9 7 4		♡ 10 2
◇ Q 8 5	S	◇ 10 9 4 3
♣ 7 3		♣ K J 10 9

♠ K 3
♡ K 8 6
◇ A 7 2
♣ A Q 8 6 5

The bidding:

SOUTH	WEST	NORTH	EAST
1 NT	Pass	2♣	Pass
2◇	Pass	6NT	Pass
Pass	Pass		

Opening lead: ♠ 8

North's Stayman 2♣ bid reveals that South has four cards in neither major, so he leaps to slam in notrump.

You see you are going to need a bit of luck, and you get some when you win the opening lead with dummy's ♠ 10 and take a successful finesse in clubs, East playing the ♣ 10 and West the ♣ 3. If you cash the ♣ A, East drops the ♣ J and West the ♣ 7. Are the clubs breaking, or should you try some other way to pick up your twelve tricks?

2. how to improve your guesswork

If East is a good player, you have to wonder why he did not drop the ♣ K — which you knew he had when the finesse succeeded — rather than its equal, the ♣ J. Is he trying a doublecross to prevent your continuing clubs, or is he being tricky with K J 10 9? You gaze at the ceiling and decide to lead a third club. Sure enough, East produces the ♣ K and ♣ 9 to defeat you.

What went wrong?

South's mistake was in leading the ♣ A to trick three.

Instead of the ♣ A, play a low one for East to win. Presumably he will make the safe return of a spade. You can test out the heart split.

If neither the hearts, nor the clubs split, you will still have the diamond finesse to fall back on for your twelfth trick. And, as the cards lie, that is the one chance in three that comes home. But before having to guess, you have tried out all three of your chances.

GUIDING PRINCIPLE: If you are testing out a suit break at notrump, whenever possible you should try to retain the controlling card in case you find out that it doesn't. Concede the trick you are prepared to lose instead of risking losing one more than you can afford.

Vulnerable: Both
Dealer: S

```
                    ♠ Q 7 3
                    ♡ A 7 6 5 4
                    ◇ 6 4
                    ♣ 8 7 6
  ♠ —                              ♠ 5 4 2
  ♡ K Q J 10 9 8 3      N          ♡ —
  ◇ 10 9 8 7         W     E       ◇ K 5 3 2
  ♣ Q 4                 S          ♣ K 10 9 5 3 2
                    ♠ A K J 10 9 8 6
                    ♡ 2
                    ◇ A Q J
                    ♣ A J
```

The bidding, or lack of it, is often the best clue to proper play.

You are South. West has preempted against your strong artificial 2♣ opening, running the risk of a double, which North is prompt to administer. However, you believe that a game with 100 honors will be more profitable, and when North's next bid is an immediate raise, you push on to slam.

Even if you recognize this situation as a familiar one, you'll need to be alert to meet this challenge.

The bidding:

SOUTH	WEST	NORTH	EAST
2♣	3♡	Dbl.	Pass
3♠	Pass	4♠	Pass
4NT	Pass	5◇	Pass
5NT	Pass	6♣	Pass
6♠	Pass	Pass	Pass

Opening lead: ♡ K

don't congratulate yourself too soon

The dummy, when it comes down, is about what South expected — spade support and the ace shown by partner's response to Blackwood. Declarer will need the diamond finesse but, from West's preemptive effort, there's a good chance it will succeed.

So South pops the ♡ A on West's ♡ K . . . and East ruffs it! Now, even though the finesse in diamonds wins, declarer can't ditch his losing club and the slam goes down.

When a vulnerable opponent preempts against a powerhouse opening bid, unless he is insane he must have a long, strong suit with which he expects to win a lot of tricks. In this case, a seven-card suit was to be expected and declarer should duck the ♡ K, conceding a heart loser for the club he'd have to lose later anyway.

Of course, declarer plays low from dummy on West's heart continuation and wins the trick by trumping. He lays down the ♠ A, and, not surprisingly, West shows out. Declarer will have to draw three rounds of trumps in order to take a club discard on the ♡ A. Therefore, he won't be able to take one diamond finesse and ruff his third diamond in dummy. Here is where the card he trumped the second heart lead with becomes mighty important. If he trumped with the ♠ 8, he'll be able to reach dummy twice, once with the ♠ 7 overtaking the ♠ 6, and again with the ♠ Q. The first entry lets him successfully finesse the ◇ J. The second removes East's last trump so that the ♡ A can be cashed and the diamond finesse repeated. Wouldn't it be a shame if declarer overcame his peril at trick one, only to lose the hand by carelessly ruffing low at trick two?

```
                    ♠ J 6 4
                    ♡ 10 5 4 3
                    ◇ A 7 3
                    ♣ Q 6 4

   ♠ 2                          ♠ K 10 9
   ♡ J 7 6 2          N         ♡ K 9 8
   ◇ Q 9 8       W       E      ◇ J 10 4 2
   ♣ J 10 9 5 3       S         ♣ K 8 2

                    ♠ A Q 8 7 5 3
                    ♡ A Q
                    ◇ K 6 5
                    ♣ A 7
```

Taking advantage of the slight chance that West held the ♣K, declarer played dummy's ♣Q but the trick was completed with the ♣K and ♣A. With only the ◇A as a sure entry to dummy, declarer had to play to avoid losing a trick in hearts or spades. So he crossed to the ◇A and . . . Take over.

The bidding:

NORTH	EAST	SOUTH	WEST
Pass	Pass	1♠	Pass
1NT	Pass	3♠	Pass
4♠	Pass	Pass	Pass

Opening lead: ♣ J

4. but what if we win?

"Two chances are better than one," grumbled South after he had led a low spade from dummy and won the finesse of the ♠Q. The ♠A failed to drop the ♠K and declarer had no way to get back to dummy to take the heart finesse which, as the cards lay, would have let him make the game.

"Too bad," sympathized North. "If you had taken the heart finesse you would have made the game."

"But if the spade finesse lost, I was giving myself a chance to get back with the ♠J and take the heart finesse later. West might have held three spades to the king just as readily as East."

West was insulted. "You remind me of the solution to Israel's financial problems that was suggested by a member of the Knesset. 'Declare war on the U.S. When we lose, they take care of everything.' A member in the back row rose to a point of information. 'But what if we WIN?'"

Assuming that each finesse has a 50% chance of success, the heart finesse is the percentage play. If it wins, that's that. If it loses, South still has a substantial chance of dropping a singleton ♠K.

As against that, in about half the cases where the spade finesse succeeds the king will remain guarded and the ♠J won't furnish that extra entry to dummy.

Why was West insulted? Suppose he has the three spades:

    ♠ K 10 3   ♡ J 7 6   ◇ Q 9 8   ♣ J 10 9 3

If South finesses the ♠Q, West simply lets him hold the trick and, unless declarer has a crystal ball and reads the position, the ♠J isn't an entry to dummy after all.

Moral: The simplest way is often the best.

Vulnerable: Both
Dealer: South

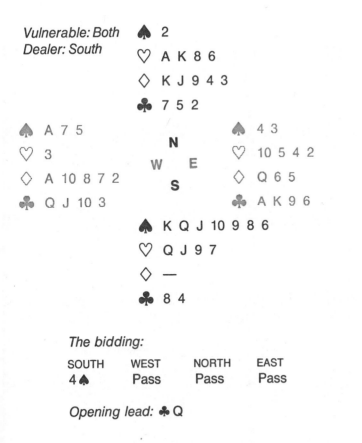

♠ 2
♡ A K 8 6
◇ K J 9 4 3
♣ 7 5 2

♠ A 7 5   ♠ 4 3
♡ 3   ♡ 10 5 4 2
◇ A 10 8 7 2   ◇ Q 6 5
♣ Q J 10 3   ♣ A K 9 6

♠ K Q J 10 9 8 6
♡ Q J 9 7
◇ —
♣ 8 4

In many deals, the key to declarer's proper play lies in the defenders' bidding. In this case, such information is not available, for neither of them has bid.

On West's opening lead of the ♣ Q, East signals encouragement by playing the ♣ 9. Next, West leads the ♡ 3, which you win with the board's ♡ A. What you have now learned about the defenders' hands should lead you to the winning play.

The bidding:

SOUTH	WEST	NORTH	EAST
4 ♠	Pass	Pass	Pass

Opening lead: ♣ Q

even though the opponents couldn't bid
5.

The taboo against preempting in one major when holding four cards in the other does not apply to seven-card suits as solid as South holds. 4 ♡ can be defeated easily in spite of "finding" a 4–4 fit; 4 ♠ should have been made. Because declarer failed to heed the clearest possible warning, it wasn't.

Although the preemptive opening made it impossible for the defenders to give any information by bidding, the first two tricks made certain things clear. It is obvious that East has both the ♣ A and ♣ K, and it is apparent that West has led a singleton heart. Surely he would not otherwise have shifted to a heart when there is the possibility that East-West may have been on the way to cashing three top clubs. Furthermore, in all probability, West has the trump ace, for without it he would not have dared to relinquish the lead at trick two.

If, at trick three, you make the mechanical lead of

dummy's trump, you will soon become a sadder and a wiser man. West will win with the ♠ A and lead to East's ♣ K. East will play a heart which West will ruff for the setting trick.

Then what do you play at trick three? The answer is the ◇ K! As you hoped, East follows suit with a low diamond and you discard your remaining club. West captures this trick with his ◇ A and hopefully leads the ♣ 3. You ruff and lead a trump. West may take his ♠ A now or later. But you have made it impossible for East to obtain the lead to give his partner a heart ruff.

What if East had produced the ◇ A to cover North's ◇ K? In that case, you would ruff and hope for the best when you lead trumps. Regardless of what the set-up might have been, your play of the ◇ K at trick three had to be your best chance.

Vulnerable: Both
Dealer: S

```
              ♠ A 6
              ♡ K 9
              ◇ J 10 8 6 3
              ♣ A 8 5 2
♠ J 7 3 2            N           ♠ Q 10 9 8
♡ 8 6 4 3      W         E       ♡ Q 10 7 5 2
◇ A 4                S           ◇ K 7 2
♣ Q 10 7                         ♣ J
              ♠ K 5 4
              ♡ A J
              ◇ Q 9 5
              ♣ K 9 6 4 3
```

Adherence to the aphorism, "Honesty is the best policy," does not always turn out to be advantageous at the bridge table. As a matter of fact, it often results in a victory for the honest man's adversary.

In this deal, you are sitting South, and West is known to you as an honest man. How do you play the hand after winning the opening lead with your ♠ K?

The bidding:

SOUTH	WEST	NORTH	EAST
1♣	Pass	1◇	Pass
1NT	Pass	3NT	Pass
Pass	Pass		

Opening lead: ♠ 2

6. not necessarily the best policy

When this deal came up in actual combat, our South declarer, upon winning the opening lead with his ♠ K, led to dummy's ♣ A and returned a club to ♣ K, hoping that the four outstanding clubs were distributed 2–2. Had they been so divided, declarer would have had nine top tricks. Unfortunately, they were divided 3–1. South next conceded a trick to West's ♣ Q, and the latter continued his attack on the spade suit. When play had ended, the defenders had made two spade tricks, two diamonds, and one club.

Would you have played the hand the same way, relying on the 40% chance that the missing clubs were divided 2–2? You should not have if you assumed that West was an honest man.

West had opened the ♠ 2, and it is accepted doctrine that one's normal lead against notrump contracts is his fourth-from-the-highest in his longest suit. Therefore, West had exactly four spades, there being three higher in his hand, and none lower. Hence, you could assume that the outstanding spades were divided 4–4, and that the opponents could develop but two spade winners.

So, at trick two, you lay down the ◇ Q, forcing out either top honor. A spade is continued, and you win with dummy's ♠ A. You lead another diamond, and that is that. You end up making two spades, two hearts, three diamonds, and two clubs.

It should be mentioned that in recent years, many of our better players have been experimenting with opening leads of the lowest card from a useful suit against notrump contracts. They are of the opinion that the time-honored lead of the fourth-highest far too often tips the scale in favor of the declarer, rather than the defenders. While one swallow does not make a summer, certainly this deal could be submitted as evidence in their behalf.

Vulnerable: None
Dealer: S

```
                    ♠ J 7 5 2
                    ♡ K J 9
                    ◇ A 9 4
                    ♣ A 6 5
♠ 8                              ♠ Q 10 9
♡ 6 4 3            N             ♡ 8 7 5 2
◇ Q J 10 5      W     E          ◇ 8 7 6 2
♣ Q 10 9 3 2       S            ♣ J 8
                    ♠ A K 6 4 3
                    ♡ A Q 10
                    ◇ K 3
                    ♣ K 7 4
```

South reached a reasonable slam contract, but lost his temper and the slam when he won the first trick with the ◇ K, banged down the two top trumps and got a bad break. "Just my luck," he growled. "Give you a spade and a club trick. Down one."

It would have been nice to drop the ♠ Q or have the trumps split but South failed to see that he might still have made the slam. How would you have tackled it?

The bidding:

SOUTH	WEST	NORTH	EAST
1 ♠	Pass	3 ♠	Pass
6 ♠	Pass	Pass	Pass

Opening lead: ◇ Q

where there's a will, there may be a way

I do not favor continuing to play a hopeless hand on the remote chance that an opponent may revoke. Neither do I believe in saving time by conceding defeat if there is any reasonable chance to avert it.

When West failed to follow to the second trump lead, it was true that East had a sure trump trick. By the same token, his possession of that card meant that he might be made to win a trick with it at a time that would be most advantageous to declarer. Saddled with one certain loser, South was wrong to concede the "obvious" club loser, when with luck and skill the bad trump break might be turned to declarer's advantage.

The first step is to cross to the ◇ A and ruff dummy's last diamond. Next you do the best you can to exhaust East of clubs by cashing the ♣ A and leading to the ♣ K. Then you win three tricks with the ♡ A, ♡ K, and ♡ Q.

(You play the hearts last because, if East is able to ruff the third heart, there is still the possibility that he began with a 3–2–6–2 distribution.)

But your main hope is that East began with exactly two clubs — or possibly only with a singleton since you have made sure if he ruffs the second club, he will be ruffing a loser. Sure enough, your faint hope is realized. East follows to all three hearts, and when you throw him in with the ♠ Q, he doesn't have a club to lead.

Lucky? Of course. The odds were that East had started with three or more clubs and that he'd be able to beat the slam by cashing a club winner. But what did you have to lose except a few minutes before playing the next deal? All South had to do was find a hope and pray and play for it to be fulfilled.

Vulnerable: E-W
Dealer: N

♠ 8 7 5 4 2
♡ A K 2
♢ 9 2
♣ Q 10 5

♠ A K J
♡ Q J 10 9
♢ 6
♣ 8 7 4 3 2

W   N   **E**
      S

♠ —
♡ 7 6 4 3
♢ Q J 10 8 3
♣ K J 9 6

♠ Q 10 9 6 3
♡ 8 5
♢ A K 7 5 4
♣ A

In rubber bridge, one should never jeopardize a game contract in order to try for the extra pittance provided by an overtrick. You are sitting South in this deal, and you win the opening lead with dummy's ♡ K.

Your challenge is to find the surefire way to make your game.

The bidding:

NORTH	EAST	SOUTH	WEST
Pass	Pass	1 ♠	Pass
3 ♠	Pass	4 ♠	Pass
Pass	Pass		

Opening lead: ♡ Q

8. for want of a nail . . .

Our actual South declarer saw no problem. (His problem came later, when North berated him for poor play, and he sought to tender a satisfactory explanation.) At trick two he led a trump off the board. East discarded a heart, and West promptly cashed three trump tricks, leaving dummy and declarer with two trumps apiece. When it subsequently turned out that the deal included a horrendous break in the diamond suit, with East having five of them, declarer eventually had to lose a diamond trick.

Without any doubt declarer got two very bad breaks. By all odds the six missing diamonds should have been divided either 4–2 or 3–3. If they were divided no worse than 4–2, declarer would simply ruff out two diamonds, and thereby establish his fifth diamond as a winner.

And, of course, if the outstanding trumps were divided 2–1, declarer's only losers would be two trump tricks, since, in this set-up, he would be able to ruff out all

three of his low diamonds.

The best South could offer was how much the existing facts defied the odds, a frequent dictum of losers. From the very beginning, declarer had a guaranteed contract, and it could cost no more than 30 points to insure it.

All he had to do was to leave the trump suit alone, and crossruff the hand. Let's say that at trick two he led a diamond to his ace, and then played the ♢ K. West would ruff with the ♠ J, after which he could cash the ♠ A K. But, dummy would still have three trumps remaining, with which to ruff out South's three low diamonds. If West declined to ruff the ♢ K, it wouldn't alter the outcome. All he could ever make would be three trump tricks, and when he took the first, he could draw no more than two of dummy's trumps.

If a subtitle were required for this deal, it would be in the form of a question: "What Price Overtricks?"

Vulnerable: Both
Dealer: W

```
                    ♠  5
                    ♡  6 2
                    ◇  K J 10 6 5 4
                    ♣  A K 9 5
♠  A K 9 7 6 2            N         ♠  J 3
♡  9 8 3                           ♡  Q 10 7 4
◇  3 2           W         E       ◇  A 8 7
♣  6 4                   S         ♣  J 10 8 2
                    ♠  Q 10 8 4
                    ♡  A K J 5
                    ◇  Q 9
                    ♣  Q 7 3
```

There is a proper time to be an optimist and a proper time to be a pessimist. Sometimes it is hard to tell which you should be.

Really, that is what your challenge in this hand is. You are South. East plays the ♠ J on the first trick and you must plan the play.

The bidding:

WEST	NORTH	EAST	SOUTH
Pass	1 ◇	Pass	1 ♡
1 ♠	2 ♣	Pass	3NT
Pass	Pass	Pass	

Opening lead: ♠ 7

when you must hope against hope

As always, you pause while you count your tricks. With good luck you can add four clubs and three hearts to your spade winner, and you still have another stopper in spades if you take the ♠ Q — but only if East can be kept off lead.

Really your only hope of winning nine tricks, therefore, lies in bringing home at least one diamond trick. So you win the ♠ Q and lead the ◇ Q, hoping that West holds the ◇ A, or that East will have the ♠ 9 so that your second stopper becomes a certainty. But wait a minute. Let's go back to the bidding and the opening lead.

West was the dealer and he passed initially. It is impossible that he did so with the ◇ A in addition to a long spade suit to the ♠ A K.

Furthermore, West's lead was the ♠ 7 — once again that all-revealing "fourth highest of longest and strongest." By applying the Rule of Eleven, you get four cards

higher than the lead known to be in the other hands, and after East's play of the ♠ J, you can see all four of them. So any hope that East has the ♠ 9 must be as vain as any hope that it is West who holds the ◇ A.

Then what hope is there that you can make your contract? The only legitimate one is that West has at least a six-card spade suit and that East began with at most a doubleton spade.

Therefore, you duck the ♠ J. East continues with the ♠ 3 and you play the ♠ 10. West wins with the ♠ K and gives you a bad moment when he does not continue the suit. You fear that East may still have a spade remaining and you may have cost yourself an extra undertrick by ducking the ♠ J. But when you get in to lead the ◇ Q, it turns out that East has the ◇ A and he does NOT have another spade. You never do win a spade trick, but five diamonds, three clubs and two hearts are more than enough to score up your game.

Vulnerable: E-W
Dealer: N

```
                      ♠  6 5
                      ♡  6 5
                      ◇  A K Q 10 9 4
                      ♣  A 5 2

        ♠  —                          ♠  Q 9 7 4
        ♡  K J 4 3 2        N         ♡  A Q 9
        ◇  J 8 7 2      W     E       ◇  5
        ♣  K Q 10 9        S          ♣  J 8 6 4 3

                      ♠  A K J 10 8 3 2
                      ♡  10 8 7
                      ◇  6 3
                      ♣  7
```

Ability to estimate one's chances is one of the major attributes of a winning bridge player.

In this deal, the opponents could have taken two heart tricks at once, but South got the favorable lead of the ♣ K and saw excellent chances for overtricks.

How would you have planned declarer's play?

The bidding:

NORTH	EAST	SOUTH	WEST
1 ◇	Pass	4 ♠	Pass
Pass	Pass		

Opening lead: ♣ K

10. when wrong thinking is right

The time for declarer to think about making overtricks is when he has already made certain of his contract. The first thing to think about is, "What can possibly go wrong? And what, if anything, can I do about it?"

The actual declarer counted on dropping the ♠ Q, playing according to the rule about finessing: "Eight ever, nine never." If the ♠ Q failed to drop, he figured to get rid of at least one heart on dummy's diamonds, so it looked like he'd make four sure, with a possibility of five, six, or even seven.

On this premise, he led to his ♠ K and West showed out! Still not panicked, declarer went to dummy with a high diamond, took the marked finesse against East's ♠ Q and cashed the ♠ A. Leaving the high trump outstanding, he led another diamond. All would still have been well if East had held even two diamonds. Declarer would throw a losing heart while East ruffed with the ♠ Q, and would lose only two hearts and one spade. But East had been dealt only one diamond. He ruffed the second diamond lead and the defense also got three heart tricks.

"Imagine," South complained, "all four trumps in one hand and a 4–1 split in diamonds, too."

Well, that's exactly what South should have imagined because it was the one possibility that could endanger his contract. To insure against it, South should finesse the ♠ 10 on the very first trump lead, making certain that if a trick was lost, a trump would still remain in dummy to cover the third heart loser.

As the cards lay, this safety play would have paid off with one of the overtricks that South had been thinking about. When the ♠ 10 holds the first trump lead, declarer goes back to dummy with a high diamond and repeats the finesse. East's ♠ Q is picked up, after which South is sure to get a heart discard on dummy's third diamond.

Vulnerable: Both
Dealer: N

```
              ♠ Q 5
              ♡ A K 10 8 4
              ◇ 7 6 3
              ♣ K Q 6

♠ A J 10 9 4          N          ♠ 8 6 3
♡ 5 2            W         E     ♡ J 7 6 3
◇ 8 5 4 2              S         ◇ K Q
♣ 4 3                           ♣ J 10 8 7

              ♠ K 7 2
              ♡ Q 9
              ◇ A J 10 9
              ♣ A 9 5 2
```

Most of us, being only human, would be delighted to share the burdens of the idle rich. But for bridge players, at least, riches should be a warning against becoming too idle. The fact that 26 points should be enough for game is no reason to relax because your lap of luxury includes 28.

You put dummy's ♠ Q on the first lead and it holds the trick. Now you have umpteen ways to make a lot of tricks, but don't let this stop you from making sure you win nine.

The bidding:

NORTH	EAST	SOUTH	WEST
1 ♡	Pass	2NT	Pass
3NT	Pass	Pass	Pass

Opening lead: ♠ J

be sure you can smile when everything goes wrong   11.

Even more worth while than the man who can smile when everything goes wrong is the bridge player who makes sure of his grin by making sure that not everything *can* go wrong. Hard luck attends this deal, but you can make it unnecessary to enjoy anybody's sympathy.

After winning the ♠ Q, declarer looked for the pleasure of some overtricks — worth $3 apiece since it happened he was playing in a rich man's 10¢ game. He cashed ♡ Q, ♡ A and ♡ K. Alas, not only did the ♡ J fail to drop, it was the danger hand, East, who turned up with the stopper. If declarer conceded a heart trick in order to set up dummy's fifth card, East's return through the ♠ K could set the contract. So declarer fell back on a second line of offense: the chance to win two or three diamond tricks.

He led a low diamond from dummy, intending to finesse. No luck: East came up with the ◇ K and South

couldn't afford to let him hold the trick.

There was still a bit of string to South's bow. The club suit might furnish four tricks if the suit broke, or if the ♣ J 10 were unguarded. But West showed out on the third club and South fell back on his last resource. Maybe East had played the ◇ K without the ◇ Q. But East won the second diamond and the defenders collected the rest of the tricks.

Tough luck? Of course. But South's riches had made him overly idle. The banker's play is to lead a heart from dummy at the second trick and finesse the 9. On half the occasions when hearts were divided 3–3, the "unnecessary" finesse would win anyway. On those occasions when South lost an unnecessary trick to the ♡ J, he could afford to be charitable. Especially since it cost a paltry 30 points to make sure of banking 600. Even at nothing per point, those are good odds.

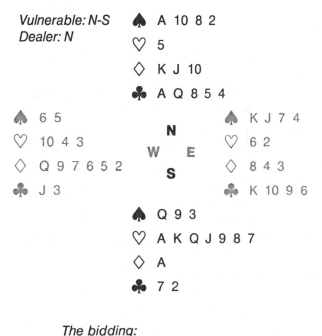

Vulnerable: N-S
Dealer: N

♠ A 10 8 2
♡ 5
◇ K J 10
♣ A Q 8 5 4

♠ 6 5   ♠ K J 7 4
♡ 10 4 3   ♡ 6 2
◇ Q 9 7 6 5 2   ◇ 8 4 3
♣ J 3   ♣ K 10 9 6

♠ Q 9 3
♡ A K Q J 9 8 7
◇ A
♣ 7 2

For declarer, bridge hands fall into three main categories: Where the contract can't be made unless the cards lie in a certain way; where one play offers a better chance of success than another; and where you don't need to care how the cards lie. In this case, South's problem is to find the sure thing.

South had no reason to regret his small slam contract, even though West's decision to open the unbid suit, diamonds, wasn't at all helpful. Indeed, South found himself with so many different chances to make twelve tricks that he even considered the prospects of making all thirteen. How would you have played it, knowing that trumps break 3-2?

The bidding:

NORTH	EAST	SOUTH	WEST
1♣	Pass	2♡	Pass
2♠	Pass	3♡	Pass
3NT	Pass	6♡	Pass
Pass	Pass		

Opening lead: ◇ 6

12. are you too proud to bet on a sure thing?

What declarer did was to draw trumps, discarding spades from dummy; then finesse the ♣Q, losing to East's ♣K. Back came a club to dummy's ♣A. South's rose-colored glasses turned a bit green when he ruffed a third round of clubs and the suit didn't break. South still had a faint hope. He ran the rest of the trumps, with a prayer that West might hold the ♠ K and the ◇ Q. No luck.

"Might have given myself a better chance," South mumbled. "Go to the ♣A at trick two, discard a club on the ◇ K, then ruff a club. If the king doesn't fall, I could take two spade finesses. But that wouldn't have worked either."

The odds on winning at least one of two spade finesses were a handsome 76%. But why settle for 76% when you can get yourself a sure thing? Do you see how?

Dummy discards clubs, not spades, on the trump leads. Now lead the ♠ 9 and, unless it is covered, let it

run. Here's the position:

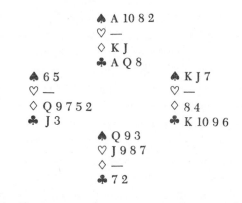

♠ A 10 8 2
♡ —
◇ K J
♣ A Q 8

♠ 6 5   ♠ K J 7
♡ —   ♡ —
◇ Q 9 7 5 2   ◇ 8 4
♣ J 3   ♣ K 10 9 6

♠ Q 9 3
♡ J 9 8 7
◇ —
♣ 7 2

Shuffle East-West's remaining eighteen cards totally at random and, unless East can conjure up a card in an unknown green suit, it will not matter how they are distributed. East can win the trick with the ♠ J, but what can he return?

Vulnerable: E-W
Dealer: W

```
                    ♠  7 3 2
                    ♡  A K 6 3
                    ◇  Q 9 5
                    ♣  Q 9 4
♠ K J 10 9 6              N            ♠  8 4
♡ 5 4                 W     E          ♡  J 10 9 8 2
◇ K J 3                   S            ◇  8 7 6 2
♣ A J 8                                ♣  10 7
                    ♠  A Q 5
                    ♡  Q 7
                    ◇  A 10 4
                    ♣  K 6 5 3 2
```

Gertrude Stein did not write, "A trick is a trick is a trick." If she had, she'd have been wrong.

The bidding was as forthright as South's problem in this deal. He needed to make nine tricks and he found the way to do so. Looking only at the North-South cards, and bearing in mind West's opening bid, would you have done so?

The bidding:

WEST	NORTH	EAST	SOUTH
1♠	Pass	Pass	1NT
Pass	2NT	Pass	3NT
Pass	Pass	Pass	

Opening lead: ♠ J

it should have been double-dummy   13.

All the key cards, ♠ KJ, ◇ K and ♣ A, are marked in West's hand by the fact that he opened the bidding and that East passed him out. Knowing this, can you make nine tricks?

Not without the club suit, of course. If you are lucky enough to find West with ♣ A singly guarded, you will have a breeze. Lead to the ♣ Q and play low on the club continuation for a "coup en blanc." The ♣ A falls on air and you can probably make eleven tricks by endplaying West in diamonds, putting him in with the third spade.

Can you improve your chances, so that you might win nine tricks if West began with three clubs? Perhaps. Do you see how?

Your initial move must be to duck the first spade. West will probably realize that you still have the ♠ AQ but no shift will be profitable. So when he continues spades, you win the trick with the ♠ Q. Next you lead a club toward dummy. If West plays the ♣ J or ♣ 10, you must hope that he began with only two, winning the trick with dummy's ♣ Q and playing the coup en blanc. But if West follows with a low club, you play dummy's ♣ 9, thereby losing the trick to the hand that cannot endanger your contract by continuing spades.

East wins with the ♣ 10 and shifts to a diamond. Of course you are not unwise enough to let this ride to dummy's ◇ Q. You go up with the ◇ A and continue clubs, establishing that suit while you still hold the spade suit stopped.

You won't make five-odd. But neither will you make only eight tricks, as you would if you played dummy's ♣ Q on the first club lead.

Vulnerable: Both
Dealer: S

```
                    ♠ A 7 4
                    ♡ J 7
                    ◇ 10 8 6 5 2
                    ♣ J 5 4

  ♠ Q J 10 8              N          ♠ 6 5 3
  ♡ 2                                ♡ K 9 8 3
  ◇ K 7 4        W         E         ◇ Q J 9
  ♣ K 9 6 3 2          S             ♣ 10 8 7

                    ♠ K 9 2
                    ♡ A Q 10 6 5 4
                    ◇ A 3
                    ♣ A Q
```

In many deals, after the opening lead is made, declarer perceives that he has optional ways of playing the hand. Usually there are just two options. This deal is peculiar in that declarer has three.

Against West's opening lead of the ♠ Q, how do you, sitting South, plan to make your contract?

The bidding:

SOUTH	WEST	NORTH	EAST
1 ♡	Pass	1NT	Pass
4 ♡	Pass	Pass	Pass

Opening lead: ♠ Q

14. everything was wrong — except South

You see four possible losers, one in each suit. Your first thought is to win the opening lead with dummy's ♠ A, and lead the jack of trumps and finesse. This will avoid the loss of a trump trick whenever East has either the K x or the K x x of trumps. But a trump trick will be lost despite two successful finesses if East happens to have three cards along with his ♡ K, or if East holds the ♡ K alone. So leading the ♡ J has only about one chance in three of avoiding the loss of a trump trick.

Then there is the possibility of leading a low club at trick two, finessing the ♣ Q. Whenever East has the ♣ K, the finesse will win, and the club loser will be eliminated. This is strictly 50-50, which is better than the poorer chance offered by attempting the trump finesse.

But the third option is the best one. *Don't* win the opening lead with dummy's ♠ A. Instead, take it in your own hand with the ♠ K, preserving the board's ♠ A as an entry. Next you play the ♣ A and continue by leading the ♣ Q, surrendering it to the defenders' ♣ K. The ♣ J is now high, and on it you can discard a loser.

The danger in this third line of play is that one of the opponents might ruff the third round of clubs. This will occur if the eight adversely-held clubs are divided 6-2 or 7-1. Mathematically, however, when eight of a suit are outstanding, 80% of the time they will be divided either 4-4 or 5-3. And in all systems of mathematics, 80% is better than 50% is better than 34%.

Possibly, as a bit of insurance, before playing clubs at trick two, you should lay down the trump ace to reduce the possibility of an opponent trumping the ♣ J with a low heart. Be that as it may, attacking the club suit immediately by playing the ♣ A and ♣ Q is the best line of play.

Vulnerable: Both
Dealer: S

```
                    ♠ Q J 5
                    ♡ K J 10
                    ◇ Q J 10 5
                    ♣ 7 5 4
♠ K 8 2                           ♠ 7 6 4 3
♡ 7 6 4          N               ♡ Q 8 3 2
◇ 8 3         W     E            ◇ A 6 4
♣ J 9 8 6 2       S              ♣ K 3
                    ♠ A 10 9
                    ♡ A 9 5
                    ◇ K 9 7 2
                    ♣ A Q 10
```

The bidding:

SOUTH	WEST	NORTH	EAST
1NT	Pass	3NT	Pass
Pass	Pass		

Opening lead: ♣ 6

As all bridge players know, every principle of play has its exceptions. The ability to recognize when to apply the exceptions is what differentiates the experts from the card-pushers.

East put up the ♣ K on the opening lead, the trick being taken by South's ♣ A.

Your goal is nine tricks and it is your move.

the rushers are the "pushers"

15.

The axiom for notrump play is to attack first the suit from which you can expect to develop the greatest number of tricks. So your "normal" play at trick two would be to lead a diamond, establishing three tricks after the defender's ◇A is driven out. But if you follow the "rule," East will win the ◇A and return a club. Whether you play the ♣10 or take the ♣A, West's club suit will become established.

In order to keep West off lead, you will try for a ninth trick via a finesse to dummy's ♡J. No luck. East returns a spade and sooner or later you must take the finesse. That too fails and you go down two tricks, which you might have held to down one had you taken the spade finesse immediately.

Before hurrying on to the next deal, muttering something about the ill luck of losing two finesses out of two, swap your self-pity for a little self-criticism. You could have insured your contract against those losing finesses.

South's correct lead at trick two is a heart to the ♡K, followed by a finesse of the ♠Q. This loses to the ♠K, but simultaneously your contract has become a certainty. If West returns either a heart or a club, you have gained an extra trick in that suit via a free finesse. You also have another stopper in whichever suit he returns. Now you can safely turn your attention to establishing three diamond winners.

Even if West makes the safe return of a spade or a diamond, you will surely win nine tricks, making as a minimum two spades, two hearts, three diamonds and two clubs.

Sometimes a guiding principle is subject to an overriding principle. Before you set up the greatest number of tricks, set up those that can safely be lost to the hand from which no danger can come. In other words, "look before you lead."

Vulnerable: None
Dealer: S

```
                    ♠ A K J
                    ♡ 7 4 2
                    ◇ A J 10 8 3
                    ♣ 6 4
     ♠ 9 7 4              N           ♠ 8 6 5 3
     ♡ A Q J 10 8    W         E      ♡ 6 3
     ◇ 6 5                S           ◇ Q 7 2
     ♣ Q 7 2                          ♣ J 10 9 5
                    ♠ Q 10 2
                    ♡ K 9 5
                    ◇ K 9 4
                    ♣ A K 8 3
```

When I saw this deal played some years ago, South as declarer put himself into a position where he was forced to guess. Actually, his contract was there for the taking.

The trouble was that South created a bogey man that could not really exist. Which should be a clue to help you avoid his error.

The bidding:

SOUTH	WEST	NORTH	EAST
1♣	1♡	2◇	Pass
2NT	Pass	3NT	Pass
Pass	Pass		

Opening lead: ♡ Q

16. the wrong time to be afraid

As the deal was played, South won the opening lead with the ♡ K. He then made the losing guess in the diamond suit. He laid down the ◇ K, after which he led the ◇ 9 and finessed against West for the ◇ Q. East produced this card and played back his remaining heart. When East failed to follow the third heart lead, South put his cards on the table and announced: "Down one," admitting that he should have finessed diamonds the other way. Which was not necessarily correct, even though East has the ◇ Q!

As North pointed out in no uncertain terms, "You threw it away at the very first trick. You should have let West's ♡ Q hold the first trick."

"I was afraid to duck," replied South. "I knew West had the ♡ A and if he stopped leading the suit, East could lead through my ♡ K and I'd never win a heart trick."

North produced the unanswerable argument. "How could East get the lead?"

If, allowed to hold the ♡ Q, West then shifted suits, declarer could take the diamond finesse into West's hand and his ♡ K would still be a stopper. Even if West produced the ◇ Q and declarer never took a heart trick, the contract would sail home with four diamond tricks, three spades and two clubs. Or if West continued hearts at trick two — even if he did not lead the ♡ A — South could win his ♡ K and take the finesse into East's hand, as he had done so unsuccessfully. But this time the finesse could not lose even if it lost.

As the cards lay, East would be heartless. And if East had another heart to lead, the hearts would have been divided 4–3–3–3 and declarer could lose only three hearts and one diamond.

If you found this hand too simple, I apologize. It's because I've so often seen a non-duck turn out to be made by a goose.

Vulnerable: Both
Dealer: S

```
                    ♠ J 4 2
                    ♡ J 9 5
                    ◇ A 6 4 2
                    ♣ K 7 2
♠ A K 10 7                        ♠ Q 8 5 3
♡ 8 7 2          N               ♡ 4 3
◇ K J 10 5     W   E             ◇ Q 9 8
♣ 4 3            S               ♣ J 10 9 8
                    ♠ 9 6
                    ♡ A K Q 10 6
                    ◇ 7 3
                    ♣ A Q 6 5
```

The bidding:

SOUTH	WEST	NORTH	EAST
1♡	Pass	1NT	Pass
2♣	Pass	3♡	Pass
4♡	Pass	Pass	Pass

Opening lead: ♠ K

If you are an experienced player, you come to recognize standard situations and learn to play them automatically. Sometimes too automatically.

After West cashes the ♠ K and ♠ A, he continues with a third spade and you ruff East's ♠ Q. You can afford to lose one diamond trick, so you need to avoid losing a club. What's your best chance of that?

after you've found a good way, look for a better   17.

You sense an old familiar theme. If the club suit splits, life is easy. But you can increase the chance to avoid a club loser by drawing only two rounds of trumps, then leading out the clubs. If everybody follows to the third round, draw the outstanding trump and concede a diamond. If someone fails to follow on the third club, you have given yourself the extra chance that it will be the player who does not have the third trump. Then you are able to ruff your losing club in dummy and you can claim your ten tricks.

However, you are running in tough luck. The clubs don't break and it is West who holds the third trump. He ruffs your ♣ Q and you still have to lose a diamond trick. Down one.

Your play was good, but it was not the best available. You don't need to rely on a club break or the lucky happenstance of finding the player with two clubs holding only two trumps. All you need is a trump break.

After ruffing the third spade, you duck a diamond. Let's assume an unfriendly defense: the opponents shift to the ♣ J. You win with the ♣ A, cross to the ◇ A and ruff a diamond with the ♡ Q. Next you lead a high trump, then cross to dummy's ♣ K in order to ruff the fourth diamond with your remaining high trump. Now you have only one trump left, but it is the ♡ 10, carefully saved to allow you to overtake with dummy's ♡ J. Dummy's ♡ 9 draws the last trump, and here is where you get rid of that fourth club. The ♣ Q is good for the last trick.

Suppose the trumps broke 4–1? Well, that would increase the chance that the player with four trumps had the doubleton club. And for the record, remember: The odds favor an uneven break of an even number of outstanding cards (i.e., the six clubs), but as close as possible to an even break of an odd number (the five outstanding hearts).

Vulnerable: Both
Dealer: S

```
              ♠ K J 7 5 2
              ♡ A K 7
              ◇ 7
              ♣ Q J 10 4
♠ ? 10 8                      ♠ ? 9 6
♡ 10 4           N            ♡ Q 8 3 2
◇ J 9 5 4 3   W     E         ◇ A 8 6 2
♣ 6 5 3          S            ♣ 7 2
              ♠ 4 3
              ♡ J 9 6 5
              ◇ K Q 10
              ♣ A K 9 8
```

You won't find the "?" in any standard deck of cards, but you will in your dreams, where the wrong card is always in the right place. (In this case, of course, the "?" in the diagram stands for either the queen or the ace.)

The opening lead of the ◇ 4 is won by East's ◇ A and he continues with the ◇ 2. South wins, and if he can guess the spade suit (assuming that it is guessable) to win a single trick, he has made his nine tricks at notrump. As South, what would you rate your chances of getting that ninth trick?

The bidding:

SOUTH	WEST	NORTH	EAST
1♣	Pass	1♠	Pass
1NT	Pass	3♣	Pass
3NT	Pass	Pass	Pass

Opening lead: ◇ 4

18. how to improve your "guesser"

The trouble is that you have only one chance to be right or wrong. If you can't pick up your ninth trick in a hurry, your opponents will win three diamonds and two other tricks to set your contract.

Now let us say that your "guesser" is working at two-to-one efficiency. That means you have a 66⅔% chance of getting your trick in the spade suit — minus the times when East has both the ♠A and ♠Q and you just can't be right no matter how you play. That still gives you better than a 50-50 chance of making the game. But why

not trade that in for about a 5 to 1 chance?

The fact is that playing the ♡ A K and leading toward the ♡ J will produce a ninth trick in that suit about 85% of the time. You win whenever the suit splits 3–3, whenever the ♡ Q or ♡ 10 is singleton or doubleton, and whenever East has any four or more hearts. Only a player so proud of his guessing ability that he'd rather guess right than make his contract any other way would give up this kind of advantage.

SOMETHING TO THINK ABOUT: Experts insist that there is no such thing as a pure guess. The implication is that there is always some clue to be picked up from the bidding or just from the atmosphere around the table. But the plain truth is that the experts' guesses are more often correct because they find a way to guess less often.

Vulnerable: None
Dealer: S

```
                      ♠  K J 10
                      ♡  8 5 2
                      ◇  A Q J 7 3
                      ♣  8 6
♠  8 7                                    ♠  9 6 4 3 2
♡  K Q J 10 9              N              ♡  7 4
◇  8 4 2             W         E          ◇  K 5
♣  K Q J                  S              ♣  7 5 4 3
                      ♠  A Q 5
                      ♡  A 6 3
                      ◇  10 9 6
                      ♣  A 10 9 2
```

The defensive play in this deal was top-notch. Declarer's play was far lower on the skill ladder. Had the play by both sides been first class, declarer would have fulfilled his contract.

West opened the ♡ K, which was allowed to win the trick. West continued with the ♡ Q and from here on it's your move.

The bidding:

SOUTH	WEST	NORTH	EAST
1♣	1♡	2◇	Pass
2NT	Pass	3NT	Pass
Pass	Pass		

Opening lead: ♡ K

how to succeed as a hold-up man

To trick two West continued with the ♡ Q, and once again declarer declined to take his ♡ A. To trick three, out of a clear blue sky, West shifted to the ♣ K.

It suddenly became apparent to declarer that he was back to where he had been at trick one. But, in the interim, West had cashed two tricks.

There was still a faint possibility that West had begun with two five-card suits, so South held off on the ♣ K for one round, winning the second club with his ♣ A. However, when South led the ◇ 10 and took the finesse, East won the trick and returned a club. So the defenders made two heart tricks, one diamond, and two clubs.

Our declarer was obviously on bowing acquaintance with the hold-up play: the refusal to win a trick in order to maintain control of the suit which an opponent has led until such time as it is safer to win the trick. But South didn't use his judgment when he permitted West's ♡ Q to

win the second lead in this suit.

As you examine the North-South hands, what is your worry? None if the ◇ K were dealt to West; you will have no problems. Your concern is that East has the ◇ K, and that he will win a trick with that card when you finesse.

Now, if East has the ◇ K, what is your worry? It is that East will return a heart, and West will slaughter you in this suit. Reflect on this possibility, and you will recognize that after ducking the first heart trick, it is really not a worry any longer.

Suppose you win the ♡ Q at trick two and take the diamond finesse, losing to East's ◇ K. If West had five hearts as the bidding suggests, East has no more hearts to lead. If East happens to have a third heart, then West started with only four. Your losers, in this case, will be just three hearts and one diamond — and that is a total you can readily afford.

Vulnerable: None
Dealer: N

♠	Q 10 7 2
♡	A K J 6
◇	Q 5
♣	K Q 4

♠ K 5		♠ 8 4	
♡ 10 8	**N**	♡ Q 4 3	
◇ K 7 6 3 2	**W E**	◇ 10 9 8	
♣ J 10 9 6	**S**	♣ A 8 5 3 2	

♠	A J 9 6 3
♡	9 7 5 2
◇	A J 4
♣	7

The bidding:

NORTH	EAST	SOUTH	WEST
1NT	Pass	2♣	Pass
2NT	Pass	4♡	Pass
Pass	Pass		

Opening lead: ♣ J

The two simplest and most widely used conventions in bridge are Blackwood and Stayman. However, the latter — aimed at locating a major suit fit opposite a notrump opening — is beginning to sprout some fancy variations. Thus, North's 2NT rebid by agreement showed four cards in both majors, with exactly two diamonds and three clubs.

Edgar Kaplan, with the South hand, deliberately chose the four-card heart fit, hoping to get a discard from North on the fifth spade. But with an immediate club loser, Kaplan had to be concerned that all three finesses might be wrong (as indeed they were). But Kaplan was able to avoid one of them. Can you equal his performance?

20. remarkable disappearance of the setting trick

In a career replete with well-played hands, this is among Kaplan's best. We've already told you that not one of the three finesses will succeed. So our congratulations if you are able to match his genius.

The obvious way to avoid losing a finesse is to avoid taking it. But in this case it is not that simple. You can be sure that when East wins the ♣Q with the ♣A he will shift to diamonds. The ◇K is offside and there is no way for South to avoid losing to the ♠K and the ♡Q. Then how did the magician cause one of his four losers to disappear?

By the simple device of refusing to cover the ♣J. One club trick would be of no use to declarer. What he needed was to keep the dangerous East hand off lead. East couldn't shift to diamonds without overtaking his

partner's ♣J, and that would give declarer two diamond discards on the ♣KQ. So the ♣J won.

West continued clubs and declarer ruffed out East's ♣A. Next he cashed two top hearts, disdaining the finesse in favor of seeing that East didn't get the lead until it was too late. Next came the spade finesse, losing to West's ♠K. But the contract was safe. West could not lead diamonds without letting declarer avoid a diamond loser. And when he led a club, North won and ran spades.

East could ruff with the ♡Q whenever he wished, but it was too late for the diamond lead. South could win with the ◇A and discard dummy's second diamond on the fifth spade. Thanks to his thoughtful play to the first trick, Kaplan had made the crucial losing trick disappear.

Vulnerable: Both
Dealer: S

```
                    ♠ 8 4
                    ♡ A K 6 4 2
                    ♢ J 9 3
                    ♣ 9 8 4
♠ K 7 3                          ♠ 9 6 5 2
♡ J 9 7 5         N              ♡ Q 10 8 3
♢ 8 4         W       E          ♢ 7
♣ Q J 10 6        S              ♣ 7 5 3 2
                    ♠ A Q J 10
                    ♡ —
                    ♢ A K Q 10 6 5 2
                    ♣ A K
```

Whether North or South is to blame for the arrival at the grand slam in this deal is immaterial. The fact is that you, sitting South, have reached a 7 ♢ contract.

Do you wish you had passed partner's leap to 6 ♢; or do you prefer to defer answering until the play has been completed? After winning West's opening club lead, what is your plan of attack?

The bidding:

SOUTH	WEST	NORTH	EAST
2 ♢	Pass	2 ♡	Pass
3 ♢	Pass	6 ♢	Pass
7 ♢	Pass	Pass	Pass

Opening lead: ♣ Q

your two chances to be a winner 21.

It is obvious that you can discard your ♠ 10 and ♠ J on dummy's ♡ A and ♡ K. The success of your contract will then depend on the 50-50 spade finesse. But if this were all there was to the hand, it wouldn't be a challenge. Is there a better line of play available?

After winning the opening club lead, you play the ♢ 10 to dummy's ♢ J, noting the 2-1 break. A low heart is then ruffed with the ♢ Q, just to make sure that West doesn't overruff. Next comes the ♢ 5 to the ♢ 9 picking up the outstanding trump in the process. Another low heart lead is then ruffed with any trump except the deuce.

That carefully-preserved ♢ 2 is next led to dummy's ♢ 3, after which the ♡ A and ♡ K are cashed. You discard the ♠ 10 and ♠ J. With both opponents following suit to all four heart leads, the board's remaining heart has become the sole surviving heart in the deck. On it you toss away your ♠ Q and you have made your grand slam.

You're probably saying that you were very lucky in finding the eight outstanding hearts divided 4-4. You sure were lucky. Mathematically, they figured to be divided 4-4 only 33% of the time. But it cost you absolutely nothing to test the hearts. If, on the fourth heart lead one of the defenders had failed to follow suit, then the other defender would have had a heart higher than dummy's remaining heart.

Wouldn't you still be in dummy, however? And couldn't you now, as a last resort, take the spade finesse? In short, wasn't the 33% chance of the eight missing hearts being divided 4-4 "on the house," with no risk involved? And, as our headline suggests, your two (the ♢ 2) chances to make you a winner?

Vulnerable: Both
Dealer: E

```
                    ♠ Q 8
                    ♡ 10 4
                    ◇ A K Q J 6
                    ♣ A K 8 2

♠ K 7 4              N           ♠ A J 9 5 3
♡ 5 3          W          E      ♡ A 8 7
◇ 7 5 4 2           S           ◇ 10
♣ 7 5 4 3                        ♣ Q J 10 6

                    ♠ 10 6 2
                    ♡ K Q J 9 6 2
                    ◇ 9 8 3
                    ♣ 9
```

The bidding:

EAST	SOUTH	WEST	NORTH
1 ♠	Pass	Pass	Dbl.
Pass	3 ♡	Pass	4 ◇
Pass	4 ♡	Pass	Pass
Pass			

Opening lead: ♠ 4

There are many occasions when it is not necessary to hear Paul Revere galloping through the night shouting "The redcoats are coming" to be warned of clear and present danger. You are alerted to your peril and your problem is to do something about it. Sometimes that something must be to rely on an enemy error, or a minor miracle.

East won the opening lead of the ♠ 4 with the ♠ J and shifted to the ◇ 10. You have another losing spade, you must surely lose the ♡ A and, at all costs, you must avoid losing a diamond ruff. Yet the play to the first trick has warned that West has — and East must know he has — a likely entry in the form of the ♠ K. Surrender?

22. when the only remedy is drastic surgery

If you win the diamond shift and knock out East's ♡ A, he will put partner in with the presumed ♠ K and ruff a diamond for the defenders' fourth trick. What to do about it?

Your only hope is to cut East's communications with West by maneuvering so that West does not win a trick with the ♠ K. You can get one pitch on dummy's second high club. You can get another if East is incautious enough to leave himself with the card that must win the third club lead.

Alas, when you lead dummy's ♣ A, it appears that East is alert to his danger. He drops the ♣ Q and continues by playing the ♣ J under the ♣ K as you take one spade discard. Well, there's still the chance that he started with just the Q J 10, but if you continued by leading dummy's ♣ 2, you are doomed to disappointment.

Although you discard your last spade, West gains the lead with the ♣ 7 and gives partner the killing ruff in diamonds.

You have forgotten that your singleton was the ♣ 9. You don't need to hope that East was dealt only three clubs — only that he was dealt the three missing honors. Lead the ♣ 8 and East is helpless. If he refuses to play the ♣ 10, you pitch your last spade and make an overtrick. If he covers with the ♣ 10, you amputate his lifeline to partner's hand by tossing your last spade.

Now East cannot get his partner in to lead that fatal diamond for him to ruff. Your contract can't be beaten. You are able to ruff East's spade lead, knock out his ♡ A, draw his remaining trumps and enjoy the high diamonds at your leisure.

Vulnerable: Both
Dealer: S

```
                  ♠ A 3
                  ♡ 5 4
                  ◇ J 10 6
                  ♣ A J 10 9 6 3
♠ K Q 10 8 4                      ♠ J 9 7 5 2
♡ A Q 3            N              ♡ 10 9 8 2
◇ 4 2          W       E          ◇ 9 7
♣ K 7 2            S              ♣ Q 8
                  ♠ 6
                  ♡ K J 7 6
                  ◇ A K Q 8 5 3
                  ♣ 5 4
```

South happily would have passed when North bid 3NT, but East had no defense and offered a vulnerable sacrifice. Indeed, this would have been set only one trick, 200 points if doubled, and would have been a good save if North-South could make 3NT.

However, you are thankful to have been driven to 5◇ because you can see when dummy is put down that you would have been held to only eight tricks at notrump.

You aren't home free yet, though. You have still to bring home your 5◇ contract. Will you make it?

The bidding:

SOUTH	WEST	NORTH	EAST
1◇	1♠	2♣	2♠
3◇	3♠	3NT	4♠
Pass	Pass	5◇	Pass
Pass	Pass		

Opening lead: ♠ K

sometimes you have to know when to swap horses   23.

While you are planning your campaign, there can be no harm in taking the first trick with the ♠ A, since you have only a singleton in your hand. But if you make this instinctive play without having thought things out, it will be too late to recover.

Let's see what happens. You draw trumps in two rounds and you need to set up the clubs. You are hoping that West may have the ♣ K and ♣ Q, so that he must win the club trick you are prepared to surrender. If not, you will have to have a favorable placement of the ♡ Q. But when you lead a club and insert dummy's ♣ 9, East wins the trick.

It doesn't take genius to know that you will be able to ruff the next spade, so East shifts to the ♡ 10. Hoping against hope, you cover with the ♡ J, but as you had good reason to fear from West's vulnerable bids, he holds both

the ♡ A and the ♡ Q and down you go.

Unnecessarily, too. A little thought instead of an instinctive play at trick one would have saved your contract. Since you must lose a club and you want to keep East off lead, why not duck the ♠ K? Now you are in a position to discard a club on the ♠ A. Even if West shifts to a trump, you win in your hand and shift your attention to clubs. You take the ♣ A, discard a club on the ♠ A and ruff a second club lead. The ◇ 10 is an entry for a third lead of clubs, which you ruff, establishing the suit. And the ◇ J remains as an entry to dummy, providing you three heart discards on North's long clubs.

By swapping a spade loser for a club loser, you have insured your contract against anything but a terrible break in clubs or finding all four missing diamonds in one hand against you.

Vulnerable: None
Dealer: N

```
              ♠ 10 9 6
              ♡ A
              ◇ A K 4 3
              ♣ A J 9 5 4

♠ A 2                      ♠ 7 5 4
♡ 10 7 3         N         ♡ J 9 6 5 2
◇ Q J 2      W     E       ◇ 10 9
♣ Q 10 8 7 3     S         ♣ K 6 2

              ♠ K Q J 8 3
              ♡ K Q 8 4
              ◇ 8 7 6 5
              ♣ —
```

There is an old and true saying in bridge: "Your bidding is only as good as your play makes it."

Whenever you get to a small slam missing the ace of trumps, you know that you must be wary not to lose another trick. And when the trump ace is opened against you, and trumps are continued, the defense may have made the going rough.

As South, would you have survived this attack?

The bidding:

NORTH	EAST	SOUTH	WEST
1◇	Pass	1♠	Pass
2♣	Pass	2♡	Pass
2♠	Pass	3◇	Pass
3♡	Pass	4♠	Pass
6♠	Pass	Pass	Pass

Opening lead: ♠ A

24. a little care or a minor miracle?

South painted a good picture of his hand, and after selecting the spade suit as trumps, North's 3♡ bid could only be read as a cue. This encouraged South to show that his spades were strong and five cards long — enough for North to bid the slam.

Declarer saw at once that if he could set up dummy's fifth club, or if the club honors dropped by the the third lead of that suit, he would have enough tricks: two clubs, five spades, including a ruff, three hearts and two diamonds. So, on winning the second trick, he cashed dummy's ♣ A and ruffed a club, returned to the ♡ A and ruffed another club, cashed the ♡ K and ♡ Q to discard dummy's small diamonds and crossed to the ◇ A to ruff still another club. Unfortunately, this plan didn't work. The clubs failed to split. To add insult to injury, East was able to discard a diamond on the fourth club lead, so he ruffed out dummy's ◇ K, forced dummy's last trump with

the lead of a good heart, and West still had the high club to set the contract two.

South had put too much faith in a minor miracle — a 4-4 club split, only 33% — when all that was needed was a more-than-twice-as-likely 3-2 break, 68%, in the diamond suit. The slam rolls home if South cashes dummy's ♡ A and ◇ A and ◇ K, then pitches a heart on the ♣ A and ruffs a club to his hand. After discarding dummy's remaining diamonds on the ♡ K and ♡ Q, a third diamond is trumped with the ♠ 10, which East cannot overruff. East can discard a club on this trick, but it won't help. South ruffs a club and still has a high trump to pick up East's ♠ 7, and an established diamond to fulfill the slam.

Perhaps the trouble was that the North hand had too many entries, while South's were less obvious. South's plan required a minor miracle; the successful one required only normal good breaks.

Vulnerable: Both
Dealer: E

```
                  ♠ K J 4 2
                  ♡ 7 6 4 3
                  ♢ A 7 5
                  ♣ A J
♠ 10 8 6 5                      ♠ 9 3
♡ K Q J 8          N           ♡ 10 2
♢ —            W       E       ♢ J 6 4 3 2
♣ 10 7 6 4 3       S           ♣ 9 8 5 2
                  ♠ A Q 7
                  ♡ A 9 5
                  ♢ K Q 10 9 8
                  ♣ K Q
```

The declarer in this deal from a team match made his teammates happy and his opponents unhappy by outplaying the opposing South to bring home a slam contract. Looking at the bidding, you might say a slam-bang contract.

South's attractive five-card diamond suit made his opening 2NT bid a reasonable choice and with no major suit fit available North's 6NT was a logical leap.

You are challenged to match South's performance against the opening lead of the ♡ K.

The bidding:

EAST	SOUTH	WEST	NORTH
Pass	2NT	Pass	3♣
Pass	3♢	Pass	6NT
Pass	Pass	Pass	

Opening lead: ♡ K

the time to break a good habit

If you are an experienced and a successful declarer, you have developed some good habits, chief among them a pause for planning the play when dummy comes down. You count your sure winners and, if you are short, you try to augment them; if you have enough, you seek a way to insure them against any foreseeable adversity.

Applying these practices to your notrump slam, you count four spades, one heart, five diamonds and two clubs — enough to deliver your twelve-trick contract without surrendering the lead. Is there anything that might diminish this total? Answer: A bad break in diamonds. How can you guard against that? You know the standard discovery play "almost without thinking about it."

Cash one of your top honors first. Then go to dummy's ♢ A. If West shows out on the second lead, you will have a proven finesse against East's ♢ J. You will lose if West has the diamond length, but you cannot guard against that unless you know positively that West, not East, is long in diamonds.

So you make the standard play dictated by good technique; you cash a top diamond in your hand and — thar she blows! No matter how you play thereafter, you cannot pick up East's ♢ J and fall a trick short.

The standard play is dictated either by a shortage of entries or by a holding that cannot provide against a 5–0 break. Neither of these is the fact here. Our successful declarer first led low to the ♢ A, intending next to play to the ♢ K. Then, if West showed out on that second lead, he would still be able to return to dummy and pick up the ♢ J. But his play successfully guarded against the 5–0 distribution that actually existed. Declarer was able to lead twice through East's ♢ J, finessing the ♢ 10 and ♢ 9 and picking up the suit without loss. Because he knew when not to play according to habit, the slam came home.

Vulnerable: N-S
Dealer: S

```
              ♠ 7 4
              ♡ 8 6 5 3
              ◇ A 9 2
              ♣ A J 6 3
♠ —                        ♠ Q J 10 9 8
♡ K Q 10 7 2      N        ♡ A J 9 4
◇ Q J 10 4    W     E      ◇ 7 3
♣ Q 10 8 7        S        ♣ 9 5
              ♠ A K 6 5 3 2
              ♡ —
              ◇ K 8 6 5
              ♣ K 4 2
```

All of us, at one time or another, have fallen victim to a horrendous trump break and have attributed our subsequent defeat to extreme misfortune. Sometimes we were justified, perhaps, but sometimes we could have overcome it.

In this deal, at trick two, you are horrified by what happens. Can you extricate yourself from impending doom?

The bidding:

SOUTH	WEST	NORTH	EAST
1 ♠	Dbl.	Redbl.	2 ♡
2 ♠	3 ♡	3 ♠	Pass
4 ♠	Pass	Pass	Dbl.
Pass	Pass	Pass	

Opening lead: ♡ K

26. hard luck plays no favorites

After ruffing the opening heart lead, you cash the ace of trumps — and West discards a heart. East is now known to have three trump winners. In addition, you are looking at a possible club loser and two diamond losers. Putting it mildly, with five or six losers staring you in the face, you are not overjoyed about your prospects, and probably wish that you "had stood in bed."

To trick two you lead to dummy's ◇ A, after which you ruff a second heart.

If you are to score both your remaining low trumps East must have four hearts. Since he is known to have five spades, the best you can hope to do is cash four tricks in the minor suits. So you test out the situation by playing your ◇ K and it lives.

Now something odd becomes apparent. Although you know you can cash only two club tricks at most, and you have the ♣ A and ♣ K, you *must* take a club finesse because you need two entries to dummy. So you lead to dummy's ♣ J and it wins. Next you ruff the third heart and lead to dummy's ♣ A, closing your eyes to see if it survives. It does! One last hurdle remains. You lead dummy's last heart and East must follow suit! You have arranged to take six trump tricks despite East's holding three sure trump winners. You don't really mind that East is able to ruff out your ♣ K.

With a little good luck and a lot of skill, you've brought home a seemingly ill-starred contract. And you're able to offer East your sympathy at *his* hard luck over failing to defeat a contract where he held three sure trump tricks and an ace in a hand where his partner had contributed a takeout double.

Vulnerable: Both
Dealer: S

```
                    ♠ 6 5 4 3 2
                    ♡ A 10 4
                    ◇ 9 5 3
                    ♣ A 3
♠ K 10                           ♠ J 9 8 7
♡ 8 2              N              ♡ 7 5
◇ Q J 10 4      W     E           ◇ K 8 2
♣ K 9 7 4 2        S             ♣ J 10 8 6
                    ♠ A Q
                    ♡ K Q J 9 6 3
                    ◇ A 7 6
                    ♣ Q 5
```

South won the first trick with the ◇ A, crossed to the ♡ 10 and took a finesse of the ♠ Q, losing to the ♠ K. The defense took two diamonds, ending with East's ◇ K. East returned the ♣ J, covered by the ♣ Q and ♣ K and won by dummy's ♣ A. Thereafter the contract proved unmakable.

Do you see a way to play the hand to insure your game against any reasonable break of the opponents' cards?

The bidding:

SOUTH	WEST	NORTH	EAST
1 ♡	Pass	1 ♠	Pass
3 ♡	Pass	4 ♡	Pass
Pass	Pass		

Opening lead: ◇ Q

a strange complaint from a partner 27.

"If only you weren't such a big card-holder!" was North's complaint — a lament more customarily heard from one's opponents than from your partner.

"Waddya mean?" South bristled. "Could I help it if the cards were wrong and the spades didn't break?"

What happened was that after the opponents cashed their two diamond tricks, they knocked out one of dummy's remaining reentries while South still had the ♠ A in his hand. (It did not really matter whether they could safely attack the ♣ A; it was sufficient to lead a second trump, even though dummy's ♡ 4 would fortuitously provide another reentry provided South had been careful to keep the ♡ 3.)

Declarer still had to return to his hand with the ♠ A, and get back to dummy to lead a third spade. When the suit failed to break, even the availability of the ♡ 4 as one more entry to dummy wasn't enough to establish the fifth spade and get back to enjoy it. South lost two diamonds, one spade and one club trick — one more than he could afford.

North's beef was because South was dealt the ♠ Q instead of a small one. Had he held a small spade, South would have simply played ♠ A and another. Dummy's three sure entries — two in trumps and the ♣ A, would have been enough to establish the fifth spade for the needed club discard. All that was required was for declarer to find the spades breaking no worse than 4–2 and neither opponent void in trumps.

Indeed, on the actual holding, declarer should first test the hearts by cashing the ♡ K. If both opponents follow, he continues with ♠ A and ♠ Q. If either defender refuses the call for hearts, the spade finesse remains as a possible tenth trick.

The moral, if I may draw one, is that a little wealth — like a little learning — may be a dangerous thing. Especially if you are unwilling to spend it in a good cause.

Vulnerable: N-S
Dealer: N

```
                    ♠ A J
                    ♡ A 8 2
                    ♢ K 3
                    ♣ J 8 7 5 3 2
 ♠ 8 7 6 4              N          ♠ 9 3 2
 ♡ 10 9 7         W          E     ♡ J 6 5 4 3
 ♢ Q 4                 S          ♢ 8 7 6 5 2
 ♣ K 10 9 6                        ♣ —
                    ♠ K Q 10 5
                    ♡ K Q
                    ♢ A J 10 9
                    ♣ A Q 4
```

This deal presented the declarer, South, with an uncomplicated problem, but one that he failed to solve. Having won the first trick with the ♡K, he crossed to dummy's ♠A to lead a club and East showed out. The clubs could not be established without surrendering two tricks to West.

If you are not already familiar with the sure winning play here, perhaps you can work it out. At any rate, you are South, resting in that 6NT contract. Comfortably, I hope. It's up to you.

The bidding:

NORTH	EAST	SOUTH	WEST
1♣	Pass	1♢	Pass
2♣	Pass	4NT	Pass
5♡	Pass	5NT	Pass
6♢	Pass	6NT	Pass
Pass	Pass		

Opening lead: ♡ 10

28. want sympathy? or do you prefer points?

The test of a bridge player's mettle — and the answer to how much of the precious metal he carries from the bridge table — is how he responds to evil breaks. Of which, needless to say, you and I seem to get more than our share.

Here you are with 34 top-card points and a good six-card suit and your slam is menaced by the outrageous club break. The actual declarer cursed his luck and played the ♣Q, losing to West's ♣K and leaving West with a sure stopper. West returned another heart to the ♡Q and South was up against the wall, needing to guess who had the ♢Q. Not unreasonably, since East was void of clubs, declarer figured that West would be shorter in diamonds. So he cashed the ♢K and took a finesse to his ♢J. South was right in his estimate of the diamond shortage in West's hand, but the shortage chanced to include the ♢Q

and down he went.

Aside from guessing the diamond finesse the other way, do you see how South could have assured his slam?

Where he went wrong was at the third trick. He should have won the first club lead with the ♣A and led a low club toward dummy's ♣J. If West comes up with the ♣K, the suit is established with only one loser, so West must play the ♣9 and allow the ♣J to win.

Now, with East known to be unable to lead a club if he wins a trick, South comes back to the ♡Q and leads the ♢J. It doesn't matter that West chances to have the ♢Q. Even if the finesse lost to East, declarer would harvest four spades, three hearts, three diamonds and two club tricks. East could not prevent declarer from winning any return on the board, and getting back to his hand after discarding his ♣Q on dummy's ♡A.

Vulnerable: N-S
Dealer: S

♠ A J 10 9 6
♡ Q 9 7 6
♢ K 6 4
♣ 4

♠ K 7 4   N   ♠ Q 5 3 2
♡ 5 2   W   E   ♡ A 4 3
♢ Q J 8   S   ♢ 5 2
♣ Q 9 8 6 2   ♣ J 7 5 3

♠ 8
♡ K J 10 8
♢ A 10 9 7 3
♣ A K 10

You and your partner have done some neat bidding to get to a good slam. Your two top clubs are going to give dummy a diamond discard. Barring misadventure, this will let you set up your diamond suit with a ruff. Your intermediate trumps are solid, except for the ace, and it is customary to concede a trick to that card in any case.

In fact, the defenders have already scored that trick and, incidentally, got off to the best defense as East took his ♡ A and led a second round of trumps. But as declarer all you need is time to rack up your twelve tricks.

The bidding:

SOUTH	WEST	NORTH	EAST
1 ♢	Pass	1 ♠	Pass
2 ♡	Pass	4 ♡	Pass
5 ♣	Pass	5 ♢	Pass
6 ♡	Pass	Pass	Pass

Opening lead: ♡ 2

not having a wonderful time ... wish I were there   29.

Declarer grabbed off his diamond discard from dummy by cashing his two high clubs. Then he played three rounds of diamonds to set up that suit via a ruff. But suddenly he found the lead in the wrong hand. He pinned his hopes on dropping the blank ♠ K Q but that pin didn't hold. So, after ruffing a spade in his hand, he found himself with a losing club that refused to disappear. If he ruffed it with dummy's last trump, he'd need to use his own last heart to get back to his hand. That would leave the ♡ 4 as the master trump. So the best he could do was draw the last trump, cash the two diamonds and concede the last club trick.

"Silly of me," South mourned. "I guess my best chance after ruffing a diamond was to come off dummy with a trump lead. Then if someone had the ♠ K Q and the ♣ Q J, I'd have brought off a squeeze while running the last trump and the good diamonds. But it wouldn't

have worked anyway."

Right as far as he went. Wrong because he hadn't looked far enough.

Twelve tricks are there for the taking if declarer makes better use of his time. His rush in setting up the diamonds led to letting down the slam. Note the difference if South ruffs his third club before leading diamonds. Next comes ♢ K, ♢ A and a ruff of the third diamond with dummy's last trump. However, South still holds two trumps to East's one. He cashes dummy's ♠ A, ruffs a spade, and has a trump left to extract East's ♡ 4. South now has two good diamonds left in his hand and he's in the right place to cash them.

Look ahead. Even if you cannot mentally play out the entire hand to its happy ending, watch out for ending in the wrong hand at the right time.

```
                    ♠ J 8 7
                    ♡ K 9 4
                    ◇ A J 6 3
                    ♣ 8 7 2
♠ K 6                              ♠ A 4
♡ J 10 2             N            ♡ Q 8 7 3
◇ K Q 10 8 7 4    W     E         ◇ 9 2
♣ 10 5               S            ♣ Q J 9 4 3
                    ♠ Q 10 9 5 3 2
                    ♡ A 6 5
                    ◇ 5
                    ♣ A K 6
```

There are times in a bridge player's life when the only thing to do is see how few tricks he can be set.

At other times, however, the declarer's problem is to find some way, however, unlikely, by which the contract can be made. Often, it is worth risking a trick to produce a miracle. But when you can find some hope without any risk, you will have achieved one of the great thrills in bridge if it comes off. You are South. Dummy has appeared and you are facing four sure losers. Be a magician if you can.

The bidding:

WEST	NORTH	EAST	SOUTH
Pass	Pass	Pass	1♠
2◇	2♠	Pass	4♠
Pass	Pass	Pass	

Opening lead: ◇ K

30. honestly, there's just no way

Your partner's free raise was a bit skimpy, and his stuff is mostly were you didn't expect it — in the diamond suit. Unless the opponents blunder badly, you can't avoid losing two trump tricks. You have one loser in hearts and one in clubs. Squeeze possibilities? Nary a hope. Establish a second trick in diamonds? How, when you know that West began with at least five diamonds including, from the lead, the king and queen?

You are tempted to surrender gracefully and get the hand over with when you are struck with the possibility of a swindle, suggested by those words "at least" in the previous sentence.

Despite your holding of only a singleton ◇ 5, you duck the first trick. You hope that West has begun with six diamonds and that East will dutifully give the count in the suit by playing his highest. Sure enough, he plays the ◇ 9.

Put yourself in West's place. It is hard for him to realize that you have given up a diamond trick unnecessarily. He thinks his partner has the singleton, so he continues diamonds and you win the trick with dummy's ◇ J, discarding a heart. When you lead a trump, East ducks and West wins with the ♠ K, returning a diamond. You play low from dummy to protect the ◇ A against a possible ruff with a low trump. You ruff in hand and lead another trump. Now, with trumps gone, when dummy gets in with the ♡ K or the ♠ J, you have the ◇ A on which to discard the ♣ 9.

What if West hadn't played a second diamond? You had nothing to lose. You could always discard a heart or a club loser on the ◇ A and the opponents would get the four tricks you were due to lose anyway.

But, as we said up top, "*Honestly*, there was just no way."

Vulnerable: E-W
Dealer: E

North:
♠ Q 9 7
♡ Q 10 8 3
♢ A 10
♣ A Q 9 7

West:
♠ J 10 8
♡ 9 7 6 4
♢ J 9 7 3 2
♣ 3

East:
♠ A K 6 4 3 2
♡ K J 5
♢ 6 4
♣ K 6

South:
♠ 5
♡ A 2
♢ K Q 8 5
♣ J 10 8 5 4 2

This deal was played in a team match and neither South brought home his contract, although it was the best one available.

Both North players chose a double as their reopening bid after East's 1♠ was passed around to them. It is close whether to bid 1NT instead, but with a maximum for that call, I think the double is slightly better since North has four cards in hearts — the other major.

Proper inferences from the auction should have led to proper play of the 5♣ contract. Would YOU have drawn them?

The bidding:

EAST	SOUTH	WEST	NORTH
1♠	Pass	Pass	Dbl.
Pass	2♠	Pass	2NT
Pass	3♣	Pass	3♡
Pass	4♢	Pass	5♣
Pass	Pass	Pass	

Opening lead: ♠ J

they ignored "the sound of silence" 31.

Both South players reached a 5♣ contract with this hand. One was thoughtless in his first play; the other's thoughtlessness occurred a little later. How would you have fared?

Both sides avoided the unmakable 3NT contract. Playing at 5♣, when West led the ♠J at one table he was allowed to win the trick, East following with the ♠2 to indicate the desirability of a shift. West found the heart shift and the contract never had a chance.

At the other table, South played dummy's ♠Q on the opening trick. East won with the ♠K and continued with the ♠A, which South ruffed. However, his finesse of the ♣J lost to the ♣K. East got out with another spade and eventually declarer had to lose a heart for the setting trick.

Winning play is to cover the ♠J, of course, and ruff the next spade. But taking the club finesse is an error.

With the ♠J and the ♣K, chances are that West would have found some way of keeping the bidding open. There was a much better chance of dropping the ♣K unguarded in East's hand, or of playing so that the contract could be made even if the ♣K did not fall.

Lead the ♣J — no harm in trying to coax a foolish cover if somehow West has the ♣K — but go up with dummy's ♣A. The ♣K does not fall, but it doesn't matter. Trump the last spade and run the good diamonds, ruffing the last if East still refuses to play the ♣K. Eventually, he must win a trick with that card, however, and now if he continues spades, you can ruff in dummy while you discard your ♡2; if, instead, East leads a heart, you let it ride to dummy's ♡Q.

Either way, you bring home your contract and prove that you should have been playing South instead of either of the players in that team match.

Vulnerable: N-S
Dealer: N

	♠ K 9 8 7 3	
	♡ A 7 3	
	◇ 5 4	
	♣ K Q 2	

♠ A 10 6 5 4		♠ Q 2
♡ Q J 9 8	N	♡ K 6 5 2
◇ 6	W E	◇ 10 9 8 7 3
♣ 7 6 4	S	♣ 5 3

	♠ J	
	♡ 10 4	
	◇ A K Q J 2	
	♣ A J 10 9 8	

The bidding:

NORTH	EAST	SOUTH	WEST
1♠	Pass	2◇	Pass
2♠	Pass	3♣	Pass
3♡	Pass	5♣	Pass
Pass	Pass		

Opening lead: ♡ Q

North had some difficulty in bidding his hand once he decided to open. His 3♡ rebid was intended to suggest a single stopper in that suit and a mild fit with partner's clubs. He did not want to bypass 3NT, but he could not be sure of running nine tricks at that denomination unless partner furnished a bolster in hearts or had solid tricks in the minors. My old friend and sometime teammate, Lee Hazen, held the South hand. He gave his partner a two-way option — game or slam — by jumping to 5♣, and North was well content to rest there.

After the heart opening, Hazen was glad he hadn't bid a slam, but the apparent certainty of winning eleven tricks did not cause him to become careless. Fair warning!

32. reminder: Murphy's Law is still on the books

It may sometimes appear that the only problem in playing a hand is "How can I lose it?" If this is the case, it will pay you to apply yourself to the discovery of the answer.

Hazen, a skilled lawyer as well as a brilliant bridge player who has twice represented his country in World Championship play, was mindful of an obscure law that isn't in the bridge rules, but ought to be. The law is "Murphy's"; briefly, it states, "If anything can go wrong, it will."

Do you see a chance to make six if West has the ♠A and carelessly ducks your spade lead after you have drawn a few trumps? Forget it. Never underrate your opponents. And don't forget about those uncharted rocks of distribution, either.

It is tempting to draw trumps, but examine your reason for hastening to do so. It can only be to avoid a diamond ruff. However, if an opponent is void of diamonds, you won't make eleven tricks, ruff or no ruff. So add another string to your bow.

Hazen did: he drew only two rounds of trumps, ending in his hand. Then he led toward dummy's ♠K. West grabbed his ace and the defenders cashed a heart. But South ruffed the third heart, crossed to dummy's ♣Q and pitched the ◇2 on the ♠K.

It might seem that this play wouldn't be necessary one time in a thousand. In fact, the odds are that six outstanding cards will divide 5–1 about one time in seven deals. But this was one of those times. On any other line of play, South loses a diamond trick and his "ironclad" contract.

Vulnerable: E-W
Dealer: S

```
                    ♠ 6 3
                    ♡ K 7 4
                    ♢ K Q
                    ♣ A K 9 8 7 5
♠ J 10 9                         ♠ Q 8 7 5 4
♡ Q 10 8 3          N            ♡ 6 5
♢ 10 7 5 2      W       E        ♢ 6 4
♣ 10 4              S            ♣ Q J 6 3
                    ♠ A K 2
                    ♡ A J 9 2
                    ♢ A J 9 8 3
                    ♣ 2
```

You may quarrel with some element of the bidding, but certainly not with the final contract. South bid 3♠ with the idea that a 3NT contract might play best if the lead did not come through North's club suit, and also to suggest his club shortage. North deliberately underbid at 4♢ so that he could show belated heart support.

When dummy came down after the opening spade lead, South was pleased with his contract. He also took pains to insure it. How would you have played?

The bidding:

SOUTH	WEST	NORTH	EAST
1♢	Pass	2♣	Pass
2♡	Pass	3♣	Pass
3♠	Pass	4♢	Pass
5♢	Pass	5♡	Pass
6♢	Pass	Pass	Pass

Opening lead: ♠ J

it's nice to have a cautious partner

Your problem is to establish dummy's club suit, because this seems to be the obvious way to avoid problems in disposing of your losing spade and possible losing hearts. (If you ruff a spade in dummy, you risk losing a trump trick; if you play hearts, you will need to find the ♡ Q or pick up the ♡ 10.)

So you win the first trick with the ♠A and start operating on the clubs. Lead to the ♣K and ruff a club and — wait a moment. You have already lost the slam, even though you have been careful not to try to cash two high clubs before ruffing.

You return to dummy with a trump lead, and ruff a third lead of clubs with ♢ 9. West could overruff, but he declines to do so. Instead, he discards a low heart, leaving

himself with one more trump than declarer. South tries to extract the trumps by cashing the ♢ AJ, but they don't split and declarer has completely lost control.

South found the simple way to make the contract against a 4–2 club split and a 4–2 trump split. He ducked the first round of clubs. East won and returned a spade. (No other return would do better.) South then took dummy's high diamonds, ruffed a second club lead and cashed the ♢ AJ, drawing trumps.

Now dummy has four good clubs and the ♡ K for reentry and South has made twelve tricks and his slam.

I heartily recommend South's bridge prescription. If you can afford to lose a trick in the process of setting up a long suit, it is usually safer to lose the first one.

Vulnerable: None
Dealer: N

	♠ 8 3
	♡ 7 5 4
	◇ K Q J
	♣ A Q J 8 5

♠ Q J 10 6   ♠ K 9 7 5 2
♡ K Q 10 9 6   ♡ 8 2
◇ 8 2   ◇ 7 6 4 3
♣ 7 4   ♣ K 2

          N
        W   E
          S

	♠ A 4
	♡ A J 3
	◇ A 10 9 5
	♣ 10 9 6 3

The bidding:

NORTH	EAST	SOUTH	WEST
1♣	Pass	2NT	Pass
3NT	Pass	Pass	Pass

Opening lead: ♡ K

Back in the early 1800's, the poet, John Keats, wrote: "A thing of beauty is a joy forever." This sentence did not relate to bridge, of course, but it really could be applicable to South's play of this deal.

West opens the ♡ K and East follows suit with the discouraging ♡ 2.

In order to succeed in South's position you have to put yourself in West's chair.

34. can you afford a little gold dust?

First, if West possesses the ♣K, you are home safely, since repeated finesses in this suit will enable you to bring home five club tricks. So you must guard against East's having the ♣K.

You would like to have West continue playing hearts, but if you follow suit with the ♡3, West will certainly not lead another heart, with East having played the ♡2. In all probability West will shift to a spade, and if East has the ♣K, you are now enroute to defeat.

Our South declarer came up with a brilliant deceptive play. On West's lead of the heart king, he played the jack! West was now convinced that declarer had started with ♡AJ alone. So, at trick two, he continued with the heart ten. South, after breathing a sigh of relief, took the ♡10 with his ♡A. He then led the ♣10 and finessed, losing to East's ♣K. It made no difference what East now returned, for South had his contract

with an overtrick: four clubs, four diamonds, one heart, and one spade.

"Suppose," you might ask, "that East had a heart to play back after winning his ♣K. The answer is, "It doesn't greatly matter." In this event hearts would have been divided 4–3–3–3 around the table, and the most that declarer would have to lose in this presumed set-up would have been three heart tricks and one club.

It is apparent that if declarer had won the opening lead with his ♡A, he would have gone down, losing four heart tricks and one club. It is equally obvious that if declarer had followed suit with the ♡3 on the opening lead, West assuredly would have shifted to the ♠Q at trick two. So the only play that could hope to win — the ♡J on the first trick — was one that could cost a trick. But it would be a trick that declarer could well afford to lose.

Vulnerable: N-S
Dealer: N

```
              ♠ Q 5 3
              ♡ Q 9 8
              ◇ A K J
              ♣ A 9 7 2
♠ 6                           ♠ J 10 9 8
♡ J 10 7 5 4      N           ♡ 2
◇ 10 9 8 5    W       E       ◇ 7 6 4 2
♣ J 8 4           S           ♣ K Q 10 3
              ♠ A K 7 4 2
              ♡ A K 6 3
              ◇ Q 3
              ♣ 6 5
```

With 16 high card points plus a couple of doubletons opposite a known 16 in North's hand, South was slam-bound as soon as he got a spade preference. But breaks were bad and South didn't know how to cope with them.

The bidding:

NORTH	EAST	SOUTH	WEST
1NT	Pass	2♣	Pass
2◇	Pass	3♠	Pass
4♠	Pass	6♠	Pass
Pass	Pass		

Opening lead: ◇ 10

knowing whence trouble can come   35.

It is sometimes difficult to plan how to play a hand when you cannot be sure from which side your contract may be threatened. But when the danger is revealed, and you know it can come from only one direction, it should not be difficult to safeguard against it when it is possible for you to do so. South had to lose a trump trick to East; that much was clear. His only problem was not to let East do any damage when he won the trick that declarer had to lose.

The ◇ K won the first trick and the ace and queen of spades, played in that order, delivered the evil tidings. There was no way South could escape a trump loser.

When West showed out on the second trump, South cashed the ♡ A and led to dummy's ♡ Q. The odds favored no worse than a 4–2 break in the heart suit, so it was rather tough luck that after East trumped the ♡ Q, there was no way for South to escape a second heart loser.

But South had no need to rely on much more than the fact that he enjoyed the favorable position of being able to play after East.

South needs to find East with no more than a single heart to insure his slam if he takes advantage of the maxim that position is everything in bridge. Instead of cashing a high heart before going to dummy's ♡ Q, declarer cashes his three diamond tricks, discarding his losing club. Then he cashes the ♡ Q and leads a second heart toward his hand. It does not matter now that East has only one heart. If he ruffs, South plays low and his heart loser disappears, so East discards. The ♣ A puts the lead in dummy for another heart lead and again declarer decides his play after East. Assuming that East discards again, declarer wins, ruffs his last heart in dummy and East can make his trump trick whenever he wishes, but not whenever he likes.

♠ A Q J
♥ J 10 6 4
♦ A J
♣ Q 7 6 5

♠ K 9 6 4
♥ K 3
♦ 9 8 6
♣ J 9 4 2

N W E S

♠ 10 8 3 2
♥ 7 2
♦ K 10 7 5 4 3
♣ 8

♠ 7 5
♥ A Q 9 8 5
♦ Q 2
♣ A K 10 3

Presented with a choice of finesses, it is up to declarer to decide which are essential.

In this deal, South might have been better off if fewer were available.

Your challenge is to play your slam to the best advantage, against the opening lead of the ♦ 9.

The bidding:

EAST	SOUTH	WEST	NORTH
Pass	1 ♥	Pass	3 ♥
Pass	4 ♣	Pass	4 ♦
Pass	4 ♥	Pass	4 ♠
Pass	5 ♣	Pass	6 ♥
Pass	Pass	Pass	

Opening lead: ♦ 9

36. one from column A; two from column B

Some deals present the same bewildering choices as a Chinese menu. This one, for example, offered three finesses. It is true that the chances are even you will win two finesses out of three. But they are also 50-50 you will lose two out of three. The conclusion: try not to take that many.

Let us assume that you are considering only the choice between the diamond finesse and the spade finesse. It should not be hard to decide that you prefer the spade finesse for a simple reason. Winning the diamond finesse will not eliminate the need to take a spade finesse later, whereas winning the spade finesse will enable you to avoid taking the finesse in diamonds.

So, quite aside from the diagnosis that the ♦ 9 appears to be a top-of-nothing lead, you don't bother with the diamond finesse. Instead, you win dummy's ♦ A and come to your hand with the ♣ K, on which East plays the ♣ 8. You lead a spade toward dummy and the ♠ J holds.

So you return to your hand with another club — but you never get there. East ruffs the second club and cashes the setting trick with the ♦ K. You have now lost considerable interest in whether the ♥ K is right or wrong.

Should you have returned to your hand via a heart finesse? Indeed not. Once the spade finesse succeeded, the heart finesse is almost surely unnecessary; certainly it is unnecessarily risky. Instead, you come to your hand with the ♥ A and repeat the spade finesse. You discard the ♦ Q on the ♠ A and now you need not care about the location of the ♥ K provided the suit divides; that is, if you first take the precaution of ruffing out dummy's ♦ J. Only then should you lead the second heart.

West wins with the ♥ K and you are happy to see that East follows because the hand is now stripped. If West leads a spade or a diamond, you can ruff in either hand and discard a club from the other. While if West leads a club, you are assured of no club loser.

Vulnerable: N-S
Dealer: S

♠ 7 5 2
♡ 8 4 3
♦ K J 10 9 5
♣ 8 2

♠ J 8 4
♡ K 10 7 6 2
♦ 7 3
♣ 9 4 3

N
W E
S

♠ K 10 9
♡ J 9
♦ A 8 4 2
♣ J 10 7 6

♠ A Q 6 3
♡ A Q 5
♦ Q 6
♣ A K Q 5

Every bridge player in this world (and other worlds, if there be such) has on occasion arrived at a very poor game or slam contract. At such times alternative courses were available to him: (1) to yell at his partner for the latter's bad bidding; (2) to throw up his hands in resignation; (3) to make the best of the resources that were bequeathed to him.

East plays the ♡ J, which you win with the ♡ Q, and in this deal . . .

The bidding:

SOUTH	WEST	NORTH	EAST
2NT	Pass	3NT	Pass
Pass	Pass		

Opening lead: ♡ 6

number three rises to the fore

When you win the first trick with your ♡ Q, you can count a grand total of only six sure tricks and you are not overjoyed at being in a three notrump contract. Where are the other three coming from?

You know that when you lead the ♦ Q at the next trick the opponents will take the ♦ A only if it is blank. After all, you opened the bidding with 2 NT so it is hardly likely that you have started with a singleton ♦ Q. In fact, when you lead the ♦ Q, West plays the ♦ 7, intending to play the ♦ 3 on the next diamond lead to inform partner that he started with an even number of cards in the suit — in this case, exactly two. So East is going to be put on notice that he needs to duck only one diamond to kill the suit and there's not much you can do about it. Or is there?

There is only one correct play to the first diamond trick. Either lead a low one to the ♦ 9, which will fool no one, or overtake the ♦ Q with the ♦ K. You must avail yourself of your only opportunity to reach dummy. East

lets the ♦ K win and you now have seven tricks.

Next you lead to your ♠ Q and the finesse succeeds. Your total of winning tricks has just soared to eight. And when both opponents follow to three rounds of spades, your remaining spade has just become your ninth and game-going trick.

If, at the completion of the play, one of the opponents turned to you and said, "You sure were lucky," you'd have to agree with him. You needed to find the ♠ K in the East hand and the six outstanding spades divided evenly so that your thirteener set up. But in the back of your mind you can also savor the thought that nobody could have played the hand any better and that you recognized your only chance to succeed.

My observation: Show me the player who is a consistent winner and you'll find that he is always called "lucky." But lots of his luck consists of locating the lucky break he needs to find to win.

Vulnerable: None
Dealer: W

```
                    ♠ K J 5
                    ♡ 10 8 3
                    ◇ A Q 10 9 8 2
                    ♣ 7
   ♠ 9 7 6                        ♠ 4 3
   ♡ A 7 5           N            ♡ K Q 9 6 4 2
   ◇ J 5          W     E         ◇ K 4
   ♣ A Q J 10 6      S            ♣ K 8 3
                    ♠ A Q 10 8 2
                    ♡ J
                    ◇ 7 6 3
                    ♣ 9 5 4 2
```

South assumed he was saving at 4 ♠, and indeed the opponents could have made 4 ♡. But after the ♡ A won and South had ruffed the next heart, he discovered that it was not impossible he could make his contract — with a little bit of luck in the diamond suit.

Declarer led to dummy's ◇ 10 and it held the trick! It now appeared that East's double was based on trump length and a singleton diamond. Take over the South seat.

The bidding:

WEST	NORTH	EAST	SOUTH
1 ♣	1 ◇	1 ♡	1 ♠
Pass	2 ♠	4 ♡	4 ♠
Pass	Pass	Dbl.	Pass
Pass	Pass		

Opening lead: ♡ A

38. when things are not what they seem

Even if East had begun with four trumps to the nine, they could be picked up, and South now counted on making an overtrick. But it took only three rounds to draw the trumps, ending in South's hand for a repeat of the diamond finesse. West played the ◇ J, North's ◇ Q covered, and to South's astonishment, East produced the only outstanding diamond — the king.

The defense then took four rounds of clubs, and declarer was −500. How about you?

Knowing that this deal was selected because it presents a challenge, you should have been warned it was tricky. But so too should the actual declarer have been alert, since East was the late John Crawford, one of the world's greatest players and a superb gambler. Crawford risked giving declarer a 100 point overtrick for a chance to set the contract — surely a good bet. But South should not have risked his contract for that self-same overtrick. Do

you see how he could guard against Crawford's coup?

When the ◇ 10 wins, South should stop and try to justify East's double. Can you guard against possible skullduggery? Yes, if you lead dummy's ♣ 7 immediately. If things are as you have figured, West can win the club and give East a diamond ruff. But then you'll be able to ruff any return and pull trumps.

Or West may instead play another heart, forcing you to ruff, in which case you attempt the diamond finesse immediately, and after East wins — whether with the ◇ K or by ruffing — dummy can win any return and you will be able to extract East's trumps and run the diamonds. As things are, East can make his surprise ◇ K, but you will now know that he did not start with four trumps since he need not have risked ducking the diamond. He could have assured your defeat by winning the ◇ K and forcing you to ruff another heart.

Vulnerable: N-S
Dealer: N

```
                    ♠ 6 4
                    ♡ A 6 2
                    ◇ 7 3
                    ♣ A J 10 9 8 5
   ♠ 8 2                          ♠ K 9 7 5 3
   ♡ Q 7 5          N             ♡ J 9 4 3
   ◇ Q J 10 9    W     E          ◇ 8 4 2
   ♣ Q 7 4 3        S             ♣ 6
                    ♠ A Q J 10
                    ♡ K 10 8
                    ◇ A K 6 5
                    ♣ K 2
```

South was a bit taken aback when North spread his puny 9-point dummy, but he admitted that even if his partner had passed initially, they might have arrived at 6NT following an aggressive 2NT opening third hand. As it was, if he could bring the club suit home for six tricks, the contract would be ironclad, even if the spade finesse lost.

You are challenged to take over, having won the first trick with the ◇ K. How would you go about winning twelve tricks?

The bidding:

NORTH	EAST	SOUTH	WEST
1♣	Pass	2♠	Pass
3♣	Pass	4NT	Pass
5♡	Pass	5NT	Pass
6♣	Pass	6NT	Pass
Pass	Pass		

Opening lead: ◇ Q

when second string is better than first   39.

Even if the club suit can be brought home without loss, South is going to have to take a spade finesse to develop his twelfth trick. The difference is that if South can win six tricks in clubs, he need have no concern about whether the spade finesse wins or loses. But is that the only difference?

The answer is no. But do you see why — and what can be done about it? Can you find another string for South's bow that will let him win the slam even if the club suit fails to run?

If the club suit produces only five tricks, you are going to need three tricks in spades — and you will need them without giving up one to the ♠ K. To give yourself this second chance, you need to find an extra entry to dummy. So, the winning play is to lead a low club and finesse, without first cashing the ♣ K. If it loses, you will be able to overtake the ♣ K and have two entries to dummy so you can take two spade finesses, assuming East holds the ♠ K. If the club finesse wins, you will be in dummy then and there and can take the spade finesse immediately.

Supposing the spade finesse loses, you will have to win the return lead in your hand, cash the ♣ K and hope the suit will run. But if the spade finesse wins, as indeed it does, you can afford to concede a club trick if necessary. Overtake your ♣ K with the ♣ A and, if the ♣ Q does not fall, force it out by continuing clubs. Later the ♡ A will give you not only reentry to the good clubs but also the entry for you to repeat the winning spade finesse.

Note what happens if you play the clubs "normally," cashing the ♣ K and finessing the ♣ J. You must still give up a trick to West's ♣ Q, but you will have only one entry to dummy. You will be unable to repeat the winning spade finesse, and down you must go.

Vulnerable: Both
Dealer: N

```
                  ♠ 5 4
                  ♡ A J 8 5
                  ◇ J 7 6 4
                  ♣ K 9 8
♠ 10                          ♠ Q J 8 7 2
♡ K Q 10 6 4        N         ♡ 9 3 2
◇ Q 10 9 5 2     W   E        ◇ K 8 3
♣ 4 2               S         ♣ 10 6
                  ♠ A K 9 6 3
                  ♡ 7
                  ◇ A
                  ♣ A Q J 7 5 3
```

The bidding:

NORTH	EAST	SOUTH	WEST
Pass	Pass	2♣	Pass
2NT	Pass	3♣	Pass
3♡	Pass	3♠	Pass
4♣	Pass	4NT	Pass
5◇	Pass	6♣	Pass
Pass	Pass		

Opening lead: ♡ K

North-South were using an artificial opening bid of 2♣ to show a strong hand, so North's response of 2NT was positive, showing at least the equivalent of an ace and a king. When North's response to a Blackwood 4NT showed the ♡ A, South bid the small slam in clubs.

Winning the first trick with dummy's ♡ A and leading to the ♠ K, on which West dropped the ♠ 10, South muttered something like, "We might have missed the boat, partner." Even if the spade suit broke 4–2, if West held the doubleton, dummy would be able to ruff two spades safely and declarer would bring home all thirteen tricks. Was there a catch?

40. birdsong from the foliage

Declarer continued by cashing the ♠ A — except that it didn't cash. West ruffed and returned a trump. This combination of bad luck and good defense was enough to prevent declarer from making his small slam. He had three losing spades in his hand and only two trumps remaining in dummy. No miracle could prevent South from losing another spade trick, and the slam contract was defeated.

North quietly agreed when his partner grumbled over the bad luck that caused him to lose a small slam on a hand that seemed to offer a good play for a grand. "But," he added, "if we had reached the grand slam, I might have been more sympathetic."

"What do you mean?" asked South suspiciously. Do you know what he meant?

Since they had bid for only twelve tricks, not thirteen, when West's ♠ 10 dropped, declarer should have been warned of the possibility of worse than a 4–2 break. He could afford the luxury of giving up a trick, perhaps unnecessarily, in order to insure his contract. How? Simply by leading a *low* spade from his hand after winning the ♠ K.

Now, even if the defenders led a trump, dummy would remain with the ♣ K 9 to take care of declarer's two remaining low spades. Then, after drawing trumps, South would still have the ♠ A to win his twelfth trick.

With the ♣ 10 outstanding, wouldn't that be dangerous? Not in the least. If West held a second spade, declarer would need to ruff only once to set up the suit. So, even if West held all the outstanding trumps, South would still make his contract if he simply guessed how to get back to his hand without leading a suit that West could overruff.

♠ Q 8 4
♡ A K 7 3
◇ 7 6 5
♣ 7 5 3

♠ K 6
♡ Q J 10 2
◇ K 10 9 8 3 2
♣ 9

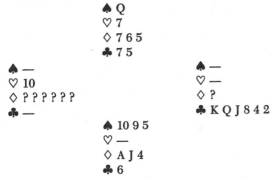

♠ J 7
♡ 9 5 4
◇ Q
♣ K Q J 10 8 4 2

♠ A 10 9 5 3 2
♡ 8 6
◇ A J 4
♣ A 6

East plays the ♣ 10 on the first trick and you (South) win the ♣ A. You hope that the ♠ A may drop a singleton ♠ K from East, but that doesn't happen and you continue spades, West winning as East follows.

West returns the ♡ Q, and the outlook isn't bright. You have already lost a spade, you have a losing club and there doesn't appear to be much hope that you can win two of your three diamonds. You cash the top hearts and lead a third one, on which East plays the ♡ 9 as you trump.

Your challenge: How can you arrange to lose only two more tricks?

The bidding:

NORTH	EAST	SOUTH	WEST
Pass	3♣	3♠	Pass
4♠	Pass	Pass	Pass

Opening lead: ♣ 9

making the most of what you know

West has failed to return a club when he got in with the ♠ K, confirming what you already suspected: East opened on a seven-card club suit. He has already followed to two spades and three hearts. West must still have the ♡ 10, so East has a singleton diamond at most and the position must be:

♠ Q
♡ 7
◇ 7 6 5
♣ 7 5

♠ —
♡ 10
◇ ? ? ? ? ? ?
♣ —

♠ —
♡ —
◇ ?
♣ K Q J 8 4 2

♠ 10 9 5
♡ —
◇ A J 4
♣ 6

Knowing West does not have another club, you consider crossing to dummy's ♠ Q and leading the ♡ 7, discarding your ♣ 3. Now if West holds the ◇ KQ, when he leads the ◇ K, you will duck and since he has nothing else to lead, he must continue diamonds, letting you score your ◇ AJ. But this won't work because when West leads a diamond, it is the ◇ 10 and East plays the ◇ Q.

You have a sure thing no matter which diamond East holds — as long as you do not let him keep it. Cash the ◇ A, then lead a club. East wins and must continue clubs. You make him a present of this trick, discarding a losing diamond. But when East leads the next club, you can throw the ◇ J while dummy ruffs. You have traded two diamond losers for one extra loser in clubs — and thus insured making your contract.

As a matter of fact, when the ◇ Q appeared you could also have endplayed West by crossing to the ♠ Q and leading the fourth heart, discarding your low club. The point was: Cash the ◇ A!

Vulnerable: Both
Dealer: S

```
                    ♠ 7 2
                    ♡ J 9 7 6
                    ◇ K J 9 3
                    ♣ A K 8
♠ Q J 10 6                          ♠ K 8 5 4
♡ Q 10 2          N                 ♡ 3
◇ 10 8 6 4     W     E              ◇ 7 5
♣ 10 5            S                 ♣ J 9 7 4 3 2
                    ♠ A 9 3
                    ♡ A K 8 5 4
                    ◇ A Q 2
                    ♣ Q 6
```

The slam in hearts was attacked at its only vulnerable spot, as West opened the ♠ Q. When South won the trick and laid down the ♡ AK, he discovered that West had begun with ♡ Q 102. The theme that brought home the contract despite this break will seem familiar — but don't get carried away.

The bidding:

SOUTH	WEST	NORTH	EAST
1 ♡	Pass	2 ◇	Pass
2 ♠	Pass	3 ♣	Pass
3 ◇	Pass	5 ♡	Pass
6 ♡	Pass	Pass	Pass

Opening lead: ♠ Q

42. cold logic versus misleading odds

Before reading further, decide for yourself how you would play this hand for twelve tricks after getting the disappointing news about the bad break in trumps.

It would have been nice if the ♡ Q had dropped — but then you might have been unhappy that you did not reach the grand slam. As it is, with the high trump outstanding and a spade loser ready to be snatched the moment the opponents get the lead, you are in some danger.

However, you can discard two spades from your hand if West has to follow to three diamonds and *two* or three clubs, so all is not yet lost. You cash the three clubs first, because with only five cards in that suit there seems less danger that one will be ruffed. But you have been beguiled by odds that do not really matter. West ruffs the third club and you have discarded only one spade loser. His spade continuation defeats the slam.

The point is that you cannot make the hand unless West holds at least three diamonds, and you cannot go down more than one if he holds only two. So you may as well give yourself the extra chance that the diamond suit is breaking favorably. Before tackling clubs, therefore, you lead three rounds of diamonds. Surprisingly enough, West turns up with four cards in that suit. So you cash dummy's fourth diamond, taking one spade discard *before* tackling the clubs. Now it doesn't matter that West ruffs the third club. Your remaining spade has gone away and instead of being minus 100 you chalk up a pleasant plus 1430 because you recognized the advantage of doing first things first.

Vulnerable: Both
Dealer: S

```
                   ♠ 4
                   ♡ A 10 7
                   ◊ Q 8 6 3
                   ♣ A Q J 7 6
♠ 10 2                          ♠ K Q J 9 7 6 5
♡ 9 6 5 4 3 2      N            ♡ K 8
◊ A J 10        W     E         ◊ 9
♣ 4 3             S             ♣ 9 5 2
                   ♠ A 8 3
                   ♡ Q J
                   ◊ K 7 5 4 2
                   ♣ K 10 8
```

Sometimes winning at bridge will depend upon figuring out who has what. But there are occasions when careful play will allow you to have no concern about locating the high cards — provided you play so that it does not matter.

Give yourself the luxury of this non-worrying situation — assuming, of course, that there is some way to make the contract after West's opening lead of the ♠ 10.

The bidding:

SOUTH	WEST	NORTH	EAST
1 ◊	Pass	2 ♣	2 ♠
Pass	Pass	3 ♠	Pass
3NT	Pass	4 ◊	Pass
5 ◊	Pass	Pass	Pass

Opening lead: ♠ 10

if all four trumps are stacked, you can't win 43.

South won the first trick with the ♠ A and ruffed a spade, to play diamonds through a possible singleton ◊ A in East's hand. But when he led a trump to the ◊ K, West turned up with the ◊ A and shifted to a heart. With a little luck the heart finesse would have succeeded or the diamond suit would have split. But, to be honest, South's play didn't merit this good luck and he lost two diamonds and the ♡ K. What went wrong?

The fact of the matter is that declarer can afford to lose two trump tricks as long as he doesn't lose a heart. So why worry who has the ◊ A? Lead up to the ◊ Q. If it loses to the ◊ A in East's hand, he can't successfully attack hearts and declarer has time to surrender another trump trick if necessary, then discard his losing heart on the good clubs.

But the ◊ Q holds the trick, East following suit. You're not yet out of the woods if you get greedy and lead another trump. All you have to do is resign yourself to losing two trump tricks, making your contract whenever West has as many as two clubs. At the third trick you lead clubs. West can ruff the third round with his ◊ J and shift to hearts but you no longer need the finesse. Go up with dummy's ♡ A and lead a fourth club, discarding your ♡ Q. You lose two trump tricks, but you've insured your contract.

TIP: PLAY TO LET THE SAFE HAND WIN THE TRICKS. Don't let a kind of safety play in one suit blind you to the danger in another. On many occasions, as this one, you can afford to lose two tricks in trumps provided you keep the safe hand on lead. Your contract was in no danger if East had the singleton ◊ A. It could be in trouble only if West gained the lead too soon.

Vulnerable: Both
Dealer: E

```
                    ♠ K 9 8 6 5
                    ♡ J 4
                    ◇ K 8 2
                    ♣ J 10 4

    ♠ 3 2                         ♠ A J 7 4
    ♡ K 10 8          N           ♡ A 6 5 3
    ◇ 7 6 4 3    W         E      ◇ 9 5
    ♣ 9 8 7 6        S            ♣ 5 3 2

                    ♠ Q 10
                    ♡ Q 9 7 2
                    ◇ A Q J 10
                    ♣ A K Q
```

Perhaps the best way to characterize bridge in a single word is that it is a game of *communications*. The word is descriptive of three different factors: information in the bidding; signalling in the play; keeping the lines open between partnership hands.

In this deal, you are South, declarer at three no trump. Your problem: to insure making nine tricks. With 28 points in the combined hands, you have two more than the theoretical 26 that will produce your game— but it isn't quite as easy as it looks. You win the club opening with the ♣ Q and it's your turn to plan the play.

The bidding:

EAST	SOUTH	WEST	NORTH
Pass	1 ◇	Pass	1 ♠
Pass	3NT	Pass	Pass
Pass			

Opening lead: ♣ 9

44. "but on the way I dropped it."

This hand looks as easy as the simple song, "A tisket, a tasket." But unless you are careful, your contract will meet the same fate as the letter to your love.

You count seven tricks in the minor suits and you are sure of at least one trick in spades. All you need do, therefore, is to take a heart trick or assure at least one additional trick in spades. How do you go about nailing down that needed ninth trick?

The declarer who held the South cards laid down the ♠ Q. East ducked and South continued with the ♠ 10. This lost to the ♠ J and East returned a club. Obviously it was futile for South to try to establish another spade trick since North held only a single reentry. He therefore led to the ♡ J, won by East with the ♡ A. Back came another club. Declarer crossed to the ◇ K in order to lead to his ♡ 9. But West was able to win with the ♡ 10 and the

defenders got three hearts, one club, and one spade, defeating the contract without even getting to cash the ♠ A.

See what happens if South makes it impossible for the defense to triumph by ducking the first spade. At the second trick, declarer leads the ♠ 10, not the ♠ Q. If East ducks, South merely continues with the ♠ Q and nothing can prevent him from winning at least two spade tricks. So East must win the second trick with the ♠ J. Assuming that he perseveres with clubs, South wins and leads the ♠ Q, overtaking with dummy's ♠ K. Now the best that the defense can do is collect two spades and two hearts. If they fail to grab their top hearts after winning the ♠ A, declarer will make three spades, three clubs and four diamonds, scoring his contract with an overtrick!

Vulnerable: E-W
Dealer: N

```
                ♠ A 8 2
                ♡ J 10 8 7 4
                ◇ A K
                ♣ J 6 3

♠ 7                          ♠ 9 6 5 3
♡ A Q 5          N           ♡ 9 6 2
◇ 8 7 5 4 3   W     E        ◇ 6
♣ K Q 10 5       S           ♣ A 9 8 4 2

                ♠ K Q J 10 4
                ♡ K 3
                ◇ Q J 10 9 2
                ♣ 7
```

South foresaw two possible menaces to his contract. After he had ruffed the club continuation on which East played the ♣ A, he considered the possibility that one opponent might have four trumps against him.

How would you play to circumvent this possibility?

The bidding:

NORTH	EAST	SOUTH	WEST
1 ♡	Pass	1 ♠	Pass
2 ♠	Pass	4 ♠	Pass
Pass	Pass		

Opening lead: ♣ K

look both ways at the crossings

South's fears were confirmed when, after ruffing the second club lead, he played two rounds of trumps, ending with dummy's ♠ A. Now if he extracted East's remaining trumps before he unblocked dummy's high diamonds, he would be unable to get back to his hand to enjoy the long cards in the diamond suit.

The solution was simple. Or so he thought. He abandoned trumps until he had cashed the ◇ A and ◇ K. Only the ◇ K did not cash. East had only a singleton diamond and ruffed the second round of the suit. He shifted to a heart and South agonized over whether to play the ♡ K or to finesse against East for the ♡ Q. This thought was both late and fruitless. It didn't matter which heart he played. West had both the ♡ A and ♡ Q and after taking them he played another diamond. East was able to over-ruff the board so the contract went down two tricks.

Cautious though he had been not to end up with the lead in the wrong hand, South overlooked one factor. He knew that if the trumps broke badly, he would be unable to ruff another club to get back to his hand, and he had tested the trump break before risking unblocking the diamonds. But he failed to realize that cashing only one high diamond would suffice to unblock the suit and still leave him with five diamond tricks.

After cashing the first top diamond, South should resume drawing trumps. Declarer's last spade would not merely remove East's last trump, it would also serve to furnish a discard in dummy. And, of course, that discard would have been the blocking diamond.

Bridge players are so accustomed to throwing losers on high trumps that the opportunity to throw a winner often hits a blind spot. As it did in this case. Or did you foresee the danger?

Vulnerable: Both
Dealer: E

```
                    ♠ J 6 2
                    ♡ K 5 3
                    ◇ J 9 8 7 4
                    ♣ 5 2
     ♠ 3                          ♠ 10 9 8 7 5
     ♡ Q J 10 8        N          ♡ 7 6 2
     ◇ 5            W     E        ◇ 10 6 3 2
     ♣ A K Q 9 7 6 4     S        ♣ 8
                    ♠ A K Q 4
                    ♡ A 9 4
                    ◇ A K Q
                    ♣ J 10 3
```

South congratulates himself when West leads the ♣ A to the second trick and East shows out. West was lurking in the bushes, hoping that a notrump contract would enable him to cash the first seven tricks.

West continues with the ♣ Q and it is now South's turn to take some voluntary action. Take over.

The bidding:

EAST	SOUTH	WEST	NORTH
Pass	2NT	Pass	3◇
Pass	3♠	Pass	4♠
Pass	Pass	Pass	

Opening lead: ♣ K

46. when generosity pays

Whenever a player has escaped one trap at the bridge table, he has a tendency to relax his efforts to evade another. South was still patting himself on the back at having reached a contract of 4 ♠ instead of 3 NT or 5 ◇ (set by a singleton club lead because East's ◇ 10 is promoted to a sure trick no matter what North does when West leads the third round of clubs). Hence, he allowed cupidity to overcome caution. He ruffed with dummy's ♠ J, making sure that East could not overruff.

This purpose was accomplished, but it proved less than admirable. All would have been well if the trumps had divided no worse than 4–2. But they proved to be 5–1, and ruffing with the ♠ J established two sure trump tricks for East — enough to defeat the contract.

South was quick to quote the odds as justification for his play. "The chances of a 5–1 break in any suit are about 7 to 1 against." North did not bother to suggest that these were the figures when the hand was dealt, but that the odds were greatly changed when it is already known that one suit has split seven-one. North simply suggested that the odds didn't favor a 720 point risk against the possibility of gaining an extra 30.

South should not have begrudged East an overruff. In fact, since declarer could afford to lose three tricks and still make the game, he should have invited it. Ruffing with one of dummy's lower spades would make the contract virtually safe against anything but a 6–0 trump break.

Whenever you play in a seven-card trump suit divided 4–3, you should give an opponent who might have length against you an opportunity to shorten himself — provided you can afford the trick this may cost.

Vulnerable: Both
Dealer: W

```
                    ♠  6 4 2
                    ♡  A 10 3 2
                    ◇  A
                    ♣  A K 9 7 6
   ♠  10 8                        ♠  K Q J 9 7 5
   ♡  K 9 4          N            ♡  Q 8 5
   ◇  Q 10 6 5 2   W   E          ◇  8 3
   ♣  8 5 4          S            ♣  Q 3
                    ♠  A 3
                    ♡  J 7 6
                    ◇  K J 9 7 4
                    ♣  J 10 2
```

When this deal arose in the 1976 Spring National Championships, virtually every North-South pair arrived at a 3NT contract, with East having overcalled in spades. To the best of my knowledge, only one South declarer fulfilled his contract. He was Mark Blumenthal, a former internationalist with the Dallas Aces.

Can you equal his success — and justify your line of play? East overtakes West's ♠ 10 with the ♠ J, and wins the trick. His continuation of the ♠ K is taken by your ♠ A.

The bidding:

WEST	NORTH	EAST	SOUTH
Pass	1♣	1♠	2◇
Pass	2♡	Pass	2NT
Pass	3NT	Pass	Pass
Pass			

Opening lead: ♠ 10

when a winning finesse must lose   47.

It is obvious that the club suit has to be attacked. The odds-on play would be to lead the ♣ J and finesse against West's hoped-for ♣ Q. Even if West possesses that key card thrice guarded, dummy's club suit will become established.

However, if you adopt this line of play, your contract will meet an early demise. East's ♣ Q captures this trick, after which East cashes four spade tricks.

Blumenthal stopped to count his tricks before embarking on the "obvious" play in clubs. Assuming that he could successfully finesse against the ♣ Q and bring home five tricks in that suit, he would still be one trick short. True, five clubs, three aces and the ◇ K counted to nine — but how was he going to get back to his hand to score the ◇ K? His ♠ A had already been knocked out, so the only possible reentry must be in the club suit. And the

only way he could hope to get back with a club was if an opponent had the ♣ Q alone or singly guarded. (Looking at dummy, no West in his right mind would cover the ♣ J with the Q-x-x or better.)

The odds were that West, not East, would be long in clubs. So the chances were that West, not East had the ♣ Q. But there was no point going with the odds if success would still spell failure. So South seized on his only real hope — that the ♣ Q would fall and the ♣ J would prove a reentry to the game-going trick.

The ♣ A and ♣ K were cashed and, as a proper reward of foresight, the ♣ Q fell. It then became routine to cash dummy's ◇ A, get to the South hand with the ♣ J and cash the ◇ K. The ♡ A was dummy's entry to the long clubs.

Vulnerable: None
Dealer: W

```
                    ♠ 7
                    ♡ A 9 7 3 2
                    ◇ 10 7 5 4
                    ♣ K 6 3
♠ 8 5                            ♠ J 9 6 4
♡ K J 8 6 4          N          ♡ 10
◇ A K J           W     E       ◇ Q 9 8 2
♣ Q J 2              S          ♣ 10 9 8 5
                    ♠ A K Q 10 3 2
                    ♡ Q 5
                    ◇ 6 3
                    ♣ A 7 4
```

The bidding:

WEST	NORTH	EAST	SOUTH
1♡	Pass	Pass	Dbl.
Pass	1NT	Pass	4♠
Pass	Pass	Pass	

Opening lead: ◇ K

On the opening diamond lead, East signals with the ◇ 9 and West continues with the ◇ K and ◇ J. East plays the ◇ 2 and ◇ 8 and South ruffs. Declarer knows that West does not open four-card majors and figures it is likely that East has begun with a 4-1-4-4 distribution. So South crosses to dummy's ♣ A, on which West thoughtfully drops ♣ J and East plays ♣ 10. The finesse of the ♠ 10 is successful and South needs his ♠ A, ♠ K and ♠ Q to pick up East's trumps. West discards ♡ 6 and ♡ 4; dummy throws ♡ 2, ♡ 3 and ♣ 3.

So far South has played excellently. But he isn't out of the woods. Take over.

48. the case of the x-ray eye

With the facts at hand, what do you know about the unseen hands? East passed partner's opening bid. He is known to have been dealt the ♠ J and ◇ Q. He is not apt to have the ♡ K, else he wouldn't have passed; besides, West has signalled in hearts so he almost surely has the ♡ K J. West must have exactly five hearts, else why would East signal for a diamond continuation if he really wanted to ruff a heart shift? With the rest of his hand counted out, you know that West started with three clubs and is unblocking that suit to avoid being thrown in with the third club and made to lead a heart.

To make your contract, you must avoid losing both a heart and a club. How? Here's the picture (see next column). Your only hope is that East's singleton is the ♡ J or ♡ 10. So you lead the ♡ Q and when East plays the ♡ K, you let him hold the trick while you hold your breath. Sure enough, East's play is the ♡ 10 and it's a matter of Q.E.D. West returns the ♣ Q to your ♣ A and

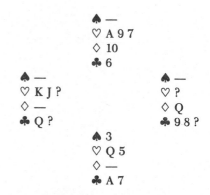

```
        ♠ —
        ♡ A 9 7
        ◇ 10
        ♣ 6
♠ —                ♠ —
♡ K J ?            ♡ ?
◇ —                ◇ Q
♣ Q ?              ♣ 9 8 ?
        ♠ 3
        ♡ Q 5
        ◇ —
        ♣ A 7
```

you lead the ♡ 5 for a finesse of dummy's ♡ 9. The finesse succeeds — it was a sure thing — and you get rid of your club loser on the ♡ A to bring home the game.

Did you "see" the ♡ 10 in East's hand? No, but you saw it in your mind's eye. It had to be where it was or you couldn't make your contract.

Vulnerable: Both
Dealer: S

	♠ J 8 5 3
	♡ K 9 8 2
	◊ J 6 5
	♣ A 8

♠ —   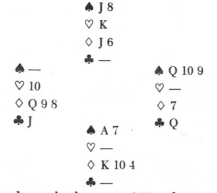   ♠ Q 10 9 4
♡ Q J 10 5 3   ♡ A 7 6
◊ Q 9 8 3   ◊ 7 2
♣ J 6 5 3   ♣ Q 10 4 2

	♠ A K 7 6 2
	♡ 4
	◊ A K 10 4
	♣ K 9 7

Any reasonable break in trumps would have made the 4♠ contract a cinch. Declarer could even play to hold his trump loser to one if West, rather than East, turned up with all the trumps. But that's not the way they were dealt.

The ♡ Q was allowed to hold. South ruffed the next heart, plunked down the ♠ K and got the bad news. East had Q 10 9 behind North's ♠ J. You are challenged to handle the cards to avoid four losers. Take over.

The bidding:

SOUTH	WEST	NORTH	EAST
1♠	Pass	2♠	Pass
3◊	Pass	4♠	Pass
Pass	Pass		

Opening lead: ♡ Q

the case of the vanishing lady   49.

On seeing the evil trump break, South cashed the ◊ A, the ♣ A and the ♣ K. Then he ruffed a club in dummy and led to his ◊ 10. The finesse went off and so did the contract. Declarer also set off a few explosive remarks about his customary bad luck, but he had only himself to blame. Did you find the better way?

Declarer had concentrated on avoiding a diamond loser when he might instead have sought a way to avoid the two "obvious" losers in spades. The winning plan required only proper timing to make one of the trump losers disappear.

Try this. Lead to the ♣ A and play another heart. East's ♡ A appears, you ruff and the ♡ K is now high. But don't let this mislead you. Cash the ◊ A, the ♣ K and ruff a club. Here's the position (see next column). If you lead the good ♡ K, East will ruff and escape the fate you have prepared for him whether or not you choose to overruff.

```
            ♠ J 8
            ♡ K
            ◊ J 6
            ♣ —
♠ —                    ♠ Q 10 9
♡ 10                   ♡ —
◊ Q 9 8                ◊ 7
♣ J                    ♣ Q
            ♠ A 7
            ♡ —
            ◊ K 10 4
            ♣ —
```

Instead, you lead to your ◊ K and return another diamond. West wins the diamond, but East cannot gain by ruffing his partner's trick so he discards the ♣ Q. Whatever West returns, North discards the ♡ K and East must trump. You put your last diamond on his ♠ 9 and the trick the black lady might have won disappears, for East must lead a trump and so wins only a single trump trick.

Vulnerable: None
Dealer: S

```
                    ♠ 8 7 3
                    ♡ K Q 10 2
                    ◇ Q J 8
                    ♣ K 9 5
♠ 10 6 4                          ♠ K 9
♡ 9 7 6 5 3      N                ♡ A J 8 4
◇ K 9 6 5     W     E             ◇ 10 4 3
♣ 8              S                ♣ J 10 6 4
                    ♠ A Q J 5 2
                    ♡ —
                    ◇ A 7 2
                    ♣ A Q 7 3 2
```

The bidding:

SOUTH	WEST	NORTH	EAST
1 ♣	Pass	2NT	Pass
3 ♠	Pass	4 ♠	Pass
6 ♠	Pass	Pass	Pass

Opening lead: ♣ 8

Perhaps you were a bit hasty in barging into slam with the South hand. There is danger that considerable heart strength might be the basis of North's positive response to your artificial 1 ♣ opening, promising 16 or more high-card points. As indeed is the case.

But you were no more hasty than West, whose opening lead of the ♣ 8 came out so fast you are convinced it must be a singleton. (It is not in any way improper to draw conclusions from your opponent's actions, although you do so at your own risk.)

Anyway, proceeding on the assumption of a singleton, it's up to you to figure how you must play to have a chance for your slam.

50. when wrong must be right

Your problem is a shortage of entries to the dummy. Unless you cover the ♣ 8 with dummy's ♣ 9, you will be conceding a club trick to East's presumed J1064. But if you play dummy's ♣ 9 so as to establish a finessing position later against East's remaining honor, you can't use dummy's ♣ K before drawing trumps. If you lead trumps from your hand, you are conceding a sure trump loser and perhaps a club ruff as well. And even if West has three trumps to the ♠ K, he can win the second trump lead and get out by leading a third spade, leaving you no way to avoid a diamond loser.

Since there is no way to avoid that diamond loser, barring the miracle of dropping an unguarded ◇ K, your best hope of making the slam is to play for the ◇ K to be "wrong"—which in this case would be right, since it is your one best chance to get to dummy. So your correct play is to cover the ♣ 8 with dummy's ♣ 9, picking up East's ♣ 10. Next you lead a low diamond!

Whether West plays the ◇ K or ducks the trick, dummy gains entry with the ◇ J. One more minor miracle is needed. East must have a singly guarded ♠ K. You lead a trump from dummy and finesse the ♠ J. The ♠ K falls under the ♠ A and you are able to draw West's last trump with the ♠ Q. Now it is safe to return to dummy with the ♣ K and lead the ♣ 5 through East's ♣ J6, picking up the suit without loss.

Your only loser is the ◇ K and because it was with West, you have brought home your optimistic slam. I am happy to give credit to Dick Miller, bridge columnist for the *National Observer*, who actually found the winning play at the table.

Vulnerable: N-S
Dealer: S

```
                    ♠ J 7 6 4
                    ♡ Q J 4
                    ◇ K 9 3
                    ♣ 10 6 3
♠ Q 2                                 ♠ 10 3
♡ 6 5 3           N                   ♡ 10 9
◇ A Q J 10 6 4  W   E                 ◇ 8 7 5 2
♣ Q 5             S                   ♣ A K 9 7 2
                    ♠ A K 9 8 5
                    ♡ A K 8 7 2
                    ◇ —
                    ♣ J 8 4
```

In a notable career, full of glee, eccentricity, and marvelous coups, this is probably Harry Fishbein's most notable hand. It is so famous that perhaps you will recognize it; nevertheless, I think it deserves inclusion in any collection of 100 most challenging hands, and I invite you to share West's brilliancy with the West cards.

You open the ♣ Q in view of partner's response and partner plays the ♣ 9, so of course you continue and are delighted when South must follow suit to both the ♣ A and ♣ K, which gives your side its book. What should you discard from the West hand?

The bidding:

SOUTH	WEST	NORTH	EAST
1♠	2◇	Pass	3♣
3♡	Pass	4♠	Pass
Pass	Pass		

Opening lead: ♣ Q

put yourself under Fishbein's beret

Fishy was famous for his berets. He probably owned as many different ones as there are hands in this book. But though imitators might fool a casual spectator, they could hope to imitate only his head *gear* by wearing a beret. It was quite another matter to imitate his head *work*. A part of that head work was devoted to making life easier for partner, even if this meant following the mule skinner's practice of walloping his mule over the head with a 2 x 4. "Does that make him obey?" the driver was asked. "Nope," was the laconic reply. "It's just to get his attention." Well, the method may be drastic, but the aim is one I recommend to any player.

You can discard a low heart on the third club and get a diamond return, or you can discard a high diamond and insist on one. But do you really want partner to lead a diamond? South has strongly bid two major suits and has turned up with three cards in clubs. If South has a diamond, you have the hand set, but can you be sure he has one? And isn't there a more certain way to score the setting trick if only you can get the message across to partner? There is, and Harry found it. He knew that partner would be most likely to return a diamond unless he could be dissuaded from doing so. So he discarded the ◇ A! Even a most obtuse East would have to be startled enough by that kind of message to realize that he did not want a diamond return. What then could he want? Obviously, a fourth round of clubs.

Did you discard the ◇ A? You not only made a spectacularly brilliant play, you also assured the defeat of the contract. No matter how he played, South couldn't shut out your ♠ Q from scoring the setting trick.

Vulnerable: E-W
Dealer: S

```
                    ♠ Q 7
                    ♡ A 9 7 3
                    ◇ 7 6 5 4
                    ♣ J 3 2
  ♠ 8 3                          ♠ 9 6 5 4 2
  ♡ 6 2            N             ♡ K 4
  ◇ A Q 8 3 2    W   E           ◇ J
  ♣ K Q 10 9       S             ♣ 8 7 6 5 4
                    ♠ A K J 10
                    ♡ Q J 10 8 5
                    ◇ K 10 9
                    ♣ A
```

The bidding:

SOUTH	WEST	NORTH	EAST
1 ♡	2 ◇	2 ♡	Pass
2 ♠	Pass	3 ♡	Pass
4 ♡	Pass	Pass	Pass

Opening lead: ♣ K

This was a most unusual deal because it included three dummies. One was plainly to
be seen; it was spread upon the table after
West's opening lead of the ♣ K. The trick
was won by South's ♣ A with East furnishing
the non-encouraging ♣ 4.

The ♡ Q was led and passed to East's ♡ K.
East returned the ◇ J and declarer made his
contract. The reader is invited to judge what
boners created the other two dummies.

52. the hand with three "dummies"

South cleverly did not cover the ◇ J with his ◇ K
and West allowed partner's ◇ J to hold. East shifted to
the ♣ 8. South ruffed and cashed the ♡ A to draw the outstanding trumps. Thereafter he ran off four top spades,
discarding two diamonds from the North hand. The ◇ Q
was conceded to West, but his ◇ A was ruffed and
declarer lost only one heart and two diamond tricks.

The second "dummy" was South. When the ♡ Q was
not covered, he should not have taken the finesse.
Instead, he should take the ♡ A and lead a second round.
Suppose West actually had the ♡ K — it would not
matter. There would be no danger that East could get a
diamond ruff for his trumps would be exhausted. The
bidding should have made it clear to South that East had a
singleton diamond, and that declarer risked losing three
diamond tricks if the trump finesse failed. Thus, if East
had started with ♡ K64, not finessing would not have
helped, but then nothing else was likely to help either.

The third "dummy" was West — for failing to overtake East's ◇ J with the ◇ Q.

What did he have to lose? After he won the ◇ Q, he
would cash the ◇ A. If East follows, South will contribute
the ◇ K and West would have to look to clubs for the
setting trick. But, of course, as the cards actually lay, East
would show out on the ◇ A and West would lead another
diamond for East to ruff, giving the defenders the setting
trick.

Perhaps you are saying, "Suppose East doesn't have
another trump?" That alibi won't wash. South cannot
have four spades, three diamonds, the ♣ A and six hearts.
That would give him fourteen cards.

Vulnerable: E-W
Dealer: S

♠ A K J
♡ Q 9 7 5 4
♢ 7 5 4
♣ A 8

♠ 6 3
♡ K J 10
♢ Q 8
♣ Q 10 7 5 3 2

N
W E
S

♠ Q 10 4 2
♡ 8 6 3
♢ J 9 3 2
♣ J 9

♠ 9 8 7 5
♡ A 2
♢ A K 10 6
♣ K 6 4

In this defensive problem, you are West. I do not really expect you to match his coup, but I have included the hand as one that you will admire even if you do not equal it.

Your opening lead of the ♣ 5 is ducked in dummy and won by East's ♣ J. His return of the ♣ 9 leaves you in no doubt that South holds the ♣ K as a second stopper. He leads to the ♡ A and by now you should have had time to think out how you will defend, so take it from here.

The bidding:

SOUTH	WEST	NORTH	EAST
1 ♢	Pass	1 ♡	Pass
1 NT	Pass	3 NT	Pass
Pass	Pass		

Opening lead: ♣ 5

what have you got to lose?

You can count South's sure nine tricks, even if his diamonds are no better than the ♢ K. He is slated to make four hearts, two clubs, at least two spades and one diamond, and for all you know he may have a few overtricks up his sleeve since once your reentry in hearts is gone, there is no hope of establishing and harvesting your long clubs.

Then where is his weak spot? The only possible one may be one that you implant in his mind. So you drop your ♡ K under the ♡ A! Your hope, of course, is that you can cause him to abandon the development of the heart suit as a fruitless path and persuade him to find one which may really turn out to be hopeless.

Put yourself in South's place after this rather astonishing turn of events. Apparently East has begun with five hearts to the J 108 and you are going to win only the ♡ A and ♡ Q. You have eight tricks on top and you need to find only a ninth. This could easily come from a successful

finesse in spades. Even if the spade finesse fails, if the suit breaks or if the ♠ 10 drops, your ♠ 9 will furnish the ninth trick. And if nothing pleasant develops in spades, there's the chance that diamonds will split, or that the ♢ Q J will fall.

So, like any reasonable South, you take the spade finesse. It loses to the ♠ Q and a spade comes back. You are beginning to despair of anything working, but you take a finesse of the ♢ 10, perhaps not your best play but nothing works. East discards a heart on the club return. The diamonds don't drop and only at the end does South discover that the heart suit would have produced four tricks after all.

The strange part of this remarkable coup is that, as West, you had nothing to lose by dropping the ♡ K. If South continues the suit, you'll still get one heart trick — which is all you could ever hope for.

```
                    ♠ A K 9 2
                    ♡ 3
                    ♢ J 2
                    ♣ 10 9 6 4 3 2

♠ Q 6 4                              ♠ J 10 7 3
♡ Q 2          N                     ♡ J 10 9 7 5 4
♢ 8 7 6 5 4  W   E                   ♢ Q 9
♣ K J 7        S                     ♣ 5

                    ♠ 8 5
                    ♡ A K 8 6
                    ♢ A K 10 3
                    ♣ A Q 8
```

You are sitting West in a game with good but not expert players. You open the top of your five-card diamond sequence against South's 3NT contract and you watch with considerable interest as dummy's ◇ J is covered by partner's ◇ Q and won by South's ◇ A.

The next two tricks look like this:

SOUTH	WEST	NORTH	EAST
♠ 5	♠ 4	♠ K	♠ 7
♣ Q	♣ K	♣ 2	♣ 5

You are confident that your partner is a more careful player than South. Take over the defense, with the added hint that there's a clue somewhere in the poem chosen for the title of this challenge.

The bidding:

SOUTH	WEST	NORTH	EAST
1♡	Pass	1♠	Pass
3NT	Pass	Pass	Pass

Opening lead: ◇ 8

54. "The Charge of the Light Brigade"

Before you lead another diamond in the expectation that partner will produce the ◇ K and let you establish your suit while you still have the ♣ J, take enough time to recite a bit of "The Charge of the Light Brigade." Also, to review the bidding.

South didn't just bid 2 NT over 1 ♠, he jumped all the way to 3 NT. For that bid he should have about 20 points in high cards and it simply isn't possible to come up with that total unless his hand includes the ◇ K. Unless that card is blank, it won't matter who holds the remaining diamonds. The suit will block if declarer wins at once. Besides, there's a strong probability that South holds either the ◇ 10 or ◇ 9 to provide another stopper.

If a diamond continuation is futile, what is declarer's weak point? He has bid hearts, and to make up his point count must have both the ♡ A and the ♡ K. And from the cards played to the club trick, you know he still has the

♣ A and ♣ 8, because East would have played high-low if he held a doubleton.

By this time you are up to the line in the poem: "Someone had blundered." You must assume that it was South and so you lead . . . the ♠ Q! You are certain to remove dummy's entry while you still hold a club stopper. If South started with three spades, he'll let you hold the ♠ Q and will make a total of three spade tricks. But in that event, the defense was hopeless anyway.

However, South began with only two spades and when the ♣ J fails to drop under his ♣ A, he winds up with only eight tricks!

Of course South should have led the ♣ A and ♣ Q from his own hand after winning the first trick. With two sure entries to dummy, even a 4–0 split in clubs could not defeat him. So, although South defeated himself, at least you helped him bring about his own downfall.

Vulnerable: Both
Dealer: N

```
                    ♠ J 9 5 4
                    ♡ 9 2
                    ◇ 10 8 2
                    ♣ Q 7 6 3

♠ A K 3 2                        ♠ Q 10 8
♡ K           N                  ♡ Q J 10 8 7
◇ Q J 9 5   W   E                ◇ 7 6
♣ A K 9 4       S                ♣ 8 5 2

                    ♠ 7 6
                    ♡ A 6 5 4 3
                    ◇ A K 4 3
                    ♣ J 10
```

A comparatively modern development in bridge is the use of "suit-preference signals" — the selection of a card in following suit or leading to a trick directing partner which suit to shift to. Like everything good, such signals are often over-used and therefore misinterpreted. Sometimes partner cannot tell whether you want a continuation of the suit led or a shift to the higher-ranking suit. In this case, however, East's card was an obvious signal.

As called for when partner leaves in a takeout double at a low level, you, West, obediently lead the ♡ K. Partner drops the ♡ Q and your ♡ K holds the trick. Take over the defense.

The bidding:

NORTH	EAST	SOUTH	WEST
Pass	Pass	1 ♡	Dbl.
Pass	Pass	Pass	

Opening lead: ♡ K

the defense gets its signals crossed

West knows that his partner has at least four good hearts, probably five. Also that declarer must have the ♡ A because if East can afford to drop the ♡ Q, he could equally afford to overtake if he held the ♡ A. So East's play is a rather obvious call for a spade shift. West therefore played the ♠ K, on which East dropped the ♠ 8 and South the ♠ 7. West continued with the ♠ A, but when East played the ♠ 10 and South the ♠ 6, it became clear that it was South who wanted spades continued. West therefore shifted to the ♣ K and got the ♣ 2 from East, so he tried diamonds, playing the ◇ Q on which East played the ◇ 6. South won with ◇ A and continued with the ♣ J, taken by West's ♣ A. The ◇ 6 looked like a come-on signal to West, so he led the ◇ 5, won by dummy's ◇ 10. The ♣ Q furnished a pitch for South's remaining low diamond and although East ruffed the ◇ A, declarer was able to scramble five tricks out of the wreckage for minus 500.

Did you, too, shift to the ♠ K, or did you read East's ♡ Q signal correctly? Reason it out. If East could afford to signal with the ♡ Q, he didn't need ruffs to promote trump tricks. He must be signalling *strength* in spades. See what happens if West leads a low spade instead of ♠ K. East wins any spade dummy plays and continues with ♡ J. Declarer's ♡ A is forced out. Now, no matter how South plays, he cannot win more than his two top diamonds. When West comes in, he again underleads the ♠ A K, putting partner on lead to extract all of South's trumps. Down four instead of only two — an 1,100 profit instead of 500.

Vulnerable: Both
Dealer: W

```
              ♠ K J 3
              ♡ J
              ◇ A Q 7 4
              ♣ K Q 9 4 2
♠ A 6 5 4              ♠ Q 10 7
♡ 8 4 3        N        ♡ 7 5 2
◇ K 9 6      W   E      ◇ J 10 5 3 2
♣ A 10 7        S       ♣ 6 3
              ♠ 9 8 2
              ♡ A K Q 10 9 6
              ◇ 8
              ♣ J 8 5
```

This deal, or one very like it, occurred in the famous Culbertson-Sims challenge match. It is not the most difficult challenge among the 100 hands you will meet in this book, but it is a deal you will enjoy if, like Josephine Culbertson, sitting West, you can manage to defeat one of the best declarers of his day, none other than P. Hal Sims. Your first test comes with the opening lead. When your partner wins a trick, he returns the ♣ 6. Carry on.

The bidding:

WEST	NORTH	EAST	SOUTH
Pass	1 ♣	Pass	1 ♡
Pass	2 ◇	Pass	3 ♡
Pass	3 NT	Pass	4 ♡
Pass	Pass	Pass	

Opening lead: ?

56. if at first you do succeed . . .

Sitting in West's chair, you are wondering where the setting tricks are coming from. Your ♣ A is sitting in front of North's opening bid in that suit and your ◇ K is probably at the mercy of North's ◇ A, since that was his second bid. South has bid hearts until the cows come home, so even one trump trick from partner seems like a remote hope. You're going to need at least two tricks from the spade suit; yet North's 3 NT call suggests he probably has the ♠ K. Laying down the ♠ A isn't going to increase the number of tricks you can get in that suit, but underleading it may put declarer to an immediate guess if your partner holds the ♠ Q.

You have now convinced yourself that desperate tactics are necessary and you lead the ♠ 4. The play to the first trick convinces you that your attack is more promising than you had hoped. After considerable thought, Hal

Sims plays dummy's ♠ 3 and your partner wins with the ♠ 10. His return is the ♣ 6, on which South plays the ♣ 8 and you win with the ♣ A. What do you return?

Does partner have a singleton club? Not likely! Does he have a sure trump trick so that cashing the ♠ A will set the contract? Most improbable. Then your best hope is to collect three spade tricks. So you lead the ♠ 5. Hal Sims glares at you suspiciously. He knows you are capable of underleading the ♠ A, or of hoping he will think so and put up dummy's ♠ K when, in fact, you have the ♠ Q.

I can only report that Sims actually played the ♠ J, losing to East's ♠ Q. And when partner returned the ♠ 7 you scored the setting trick with the ♠ A. Plus a grudging "Nice play" from your opponent. Remember, however, the caution against taking the pitcher to the well too often. Try again only when nothing else will serve.

(N-S 60 part-score)
Vulnerable: N-S
Dealer: S

```
                   ♠ Q 5
                   ♡ Q 3
                   ◇ Q J 8 7 5 4
                   ♣ A J 9
♠ K 9                              ♠ 6 4
♡ A K 9 8 4         N              ♡ 10 7 6 5
◇ K 9 3        W         E         ◇ 10 6
♣ 10 6 2            S              ♣ Q 8 7 4 3
                   ♠ A J 10 8 7 3 2
                   ♡ J 2
                   ◇ A 2
                   ♣ K 5
```

I am indebted to Aksel J. Nielsen of Copenhagen for reminding me, by publication of a similar diagram in his recent book, of a deal of many years ago in which I occupied the West chair, defending against South's contract of 4♠.

I opened the ♡ K, on which my favorite partner, the late Helen Sobel Smith, played the ♡ 6. I continued with the ♡ A, partner playing the ♡ 5. South's cards were the ♡ 2 and ♡ J. I invite you to share my problem: How to find the winning defense.

The bidding:

SOUTH	WEST	NORTH	EAST
1 ♠	Dbl.	2 ◇	2 ♡
2 ♠	3 ♡	3 ♠	Pass
Pass	4 ♡	Pass	Pass
4 ♠	Pass	Pass	Pass

Opening lead: ♡ K

play them close to the vest

Too often, most of us play as if the enemy knew as much about our cards as we do, looking right at them. The fact is that, if you hold your cards reasonably close to the chest (ladies who are generously endowed may have to sit a bit further back from the table), you will have a reasonably good chance of getting away with an apparently suicidal play. Not that I recommend such tactics if a better scheme offers itself.

Could I continue hearts with reasonable safety? Could East have scraped up a bid with only three to the ♡ 10? Hardly, for she had echoed, telling me she held four.

And what did South hold? To justify his three bids, South needed considerable spade length, and surely the ◇ A and no doubt the ♣ K as well. It was likely that because of the score and vulnerability partner had

scraped up some sort of bid on the proverbial "smell-of-an-oil rag" and a couple of distributional points. But declarer could hardly know that.

So I led the ♠ 9 to the third trick. Declarer happily played dummy's ♠ Q and looked scornful when East failed to produce the ♠ K. The ♠ 5 was continued and when East played another low card, South confidently took a finesse against the missing ♠ K. I don't blame him, though his partner did.

On winning the ♠ K, it was safe to continue hearts since dummy didn't have another trump. In the end, declarer could choose to be defeated by taking either a club or a diamond finesse. But win the hand he could not. Though, as you will observe, any lead but the ♠ 9 at trick three would have assured declarer's contract.

Vulnerable: Both
Dealer: W

	♠ A K 8 2	
	♡ A K 4 2	
	◇ Q 6	
	♣ 6 5 2	

♠ 6 5		♠ 10 9 4 3
♡ J 8 6	**N**	♡ 10 3
◇ A K J 8 7 3	**W E**	◇ 9 2
♣ A 9	**S**	♣ K J 10 8 3

	♠ Q J 7	
	♡ Q 9 7 5	
	◇ 10 5 4	
	♣ Q 7 4	

Let's turn the clock back some 25 years, to the 1951 National Open Team-of-Four Championships. I am your partner, sitting East. You are occupying the West seat, actually held by my favorite partner, the late Helen Sobel Smith, one of the world's top players. We are defending against South's 2♡ partscore contract.

Let's see if you can defend as well as Helen did.

The bidding:

WEST	NORTH	EAST	SOUTH
1◇	Dbl.	Pass	1♡
Pass	2♡	Pass	Pass
Pass			

Opening lead: ◇ K

58. this lady was a trump!

On your ◇ K, I play the ◇ 9. You continue with the ◇ A, on which I complete the echo by dropping the ◇ 2. To trick three you lead the high ◇ J, and dummy discards the ♣ 2. I toss out the ♣ 8. What do you lead?

If you now play the ♣ A and follow up by leading to my ♣ K, we will have taken the first five tricks. But we won't get any more no matter what I return.

It didn't take Helen very long to come up with the winning play at trick four. She recognized that I probably had the ♣ K — and she led the ♣ 9, underleading her ♣ A! I won the trick with the king (I must admit, a bit surprised), and made haste to lead back to Helen's ♣ A.

At this point her far-sighted plan became clear, for her next play was a fourth diamond. Dummy discarded a

spade, and I delivered an uppercut with the trump 10, which South overruffed with the ♡ Q. Helen, with the J86 of trumps over South's 975, now had herself a sure trump winner, and the setting trick.

How did Helen know that I had the 10 of trumps — or, for that matter, that I had the ♣ K? She didn't, although my discard of the ♣ 8 seemed to indicate that I had the latter card. She simply hoped that I had the ♡ 10, and saw that if I did, she could defeat the contract.

If you didn't defend as Helen did, don't feel too bad. When the deal was replayed, our partners also arrived at a 2 ♡ contract. But the West defender — a fine player — after cashing three diamond tricks, led the ♣ A — and the 2 ♡ contract was fulfilled.

Vulnerable: Both
Dealer: S

```
              ♠ 7 5 4 2
              ♡ 6 5
              ◇ 8 4 2
              ♣ J 8 7 4

♠ J 10 9 6              ♠ K 8 3
♡ K 8 4 2       N       ♡ J 3
◇ J 7 5 3    W   E      ◇ Q 10 9 6
♣ 5             S       ♣ 9 6 3 2

              ♠ A Q
              ♡ A Q 10 9 7
              ◇ A K
              ♣ A K Q 10
```

The bidding:

SOUTH	WEST	NORTH	EAST
2♣	Pass	2◇	Pass
2♡	Pass	2NT	Pass
3♣	Pass	4♣	Pass
6♣	Pass	Pass	Pass

Opening lead: ♠ J

It is as important for the defenders to visualize declarer's hand as it is for declarer to count out his opponents' probable distribution. What's more, the defenders have to do it faster, for declarer can take his time without giving anything away.

As West in this deal, you are going to need to use your wits to the utmost to produce even the remotest chance of defeating the slam. East plays the ♠ K on the first trick and South wins with the ♠ A. He cashes the ♣ A and leads the ♣ 10, overtaking with North's ♣ J, while you drop the ◇ 3. Next South finesses the ♡ Q. By now you should have laid your plans.

how to build a Trojan horse   59.

If you have been thinking about the bidding, you know that partner has only one more heart and no matter which it is, after you have taken the ♡ K, South must have a solid heart suit. Obviously, he has the ♠ Q and the ◇ A, since he was missing the ♡ K and the ♠ K and still bid a slam virtually on his own. Having reasoned thus far — and assuming you have been able to do so fast — you duck the ♡ Q!

Your hope is that South started with only four clubs. If partner has four, you know these include the ♣ 9. And the most you are risking is a 20-point overtrick.

South quite properly continues with the ♡ A, since if East has started with four or more hearts, declarer will need to ruff at least once in dummy. But East's ♡ J drops under the ♡ A. Greedily, South leads a low heart, hoping to ruff out East's ♡ K. But when dummy ruffs, East overruffs with the ♣ 9 and returns a club, removing dummy's

last trump. West's ♡ K has now become the setting trick.

What a wonderful investment West made — a 20-point overtrick returning a profit of 1470, roughly 75 to 1. West can truly congratulate himself on a brilliant play, but South must call himself a greedy loser if North has not already made that point.

When the ♡ J dropped, South didn't need to pursue a 20-point overtrick. As I have previously observed, it isn't worth 75 to 1 to bet against the possibility that a player hasn't accidentally pulled the wrong card.

With all suits controlled, South should have drawn the trumps and conceded a trick to the ♡ K. Even if such concession proved to be unnecessary, South could afford to be generous.

Vulnerable: Both
Dealer: S

```
                    ♠ A 2
                    ♡ 10 9 5
                    ♢ A J 6 5
                    ♣ A Q 10 9
 ♠ Q 9 7 5                        ♠ K 10 8 6 4
 ♡ A Q 8          N               ♡ 6 4
 ♢ Q 8 7 4     W     E            ♢ 9 3 2
 ♣ 7 5            S               ♣ K 8 4
                    ♠ J 3
                    ♡ K J 7 3 2
                    ♢ K 10
                    ♣ J 6 3 2
```

The bidding:

SOUTH	WEST	NORTH	EAST
Pass	Pass	1♣	Pass
1♡	Pass	2♡	Pass
3♣	Pass	3NT	Pass
4♡	Pass	Pass	Pass

Opening lead: ♣ 7

The losing defender gives his opponent no chance to blow his contract. The winner tries to find ways to persuade the declarer that he has a "better" play. Put yourself in West's place and decide whether you would be a winner or a loser.

Declarer finessed in clubs, losing to the ♣ K. East returned the ♣ 8 as a signal that his reentry was in the higher ranking suit, spades. Dummy won and lost a heart finesse to the ♡ Q. West obediently returned a spade and declarer went up with dummy's ♠ A, crossed to the ♢ K, took a winning finesse of the ♢ J and discarded the ♠ J on the ♢ A. Then he forced out the ♡ A, losing only one club and two trump tricks.

What went wrong?

60. give your opponent a chance . . . to go wrong

As declarer, you probably observe the advice to take your time when dummy comes down and make your plan before you make your first play. The time that declarer uses for this purpose should also be used by the defenders so that, so far as possible, they are aware of declarer's problem, if any.

While South was deciding how to play the hand, West should have been reconstructing South's hand by reviewing the bidding, and deciding how the contract might be set. West should know that South has exactly five hearts; with four, he'd have left the contract at three notrump; with six, he'd have jumped to game instead of bothering to raise partner's clubs. When declarer finessed in clubs and East produced the ♣ K and returned the ♣ 8 — a suit preference signal for a spade play whenever West got the lead — it was obvious that South simply had to have the ♢ K to justify his try for game.

Obviously, if the South hand included more than one spade and West won the first trump lead with the ♡ Q, declarer would have no hope but to finesse the ♢ J in order to get a spade discard. How could West persuade him not to make the winning play? By winning the first trump trick with the ♡ A, convincing South that a dangerous diamond finesse would run an unnecessary risk.

So West wins with the ♡ A and leads a spade. South takes dummy's ♠ A and plays for the "sure thing" — a repeat finesse in trumps to pick up East's ♡ Q. But West produces that card, puts partner in with the ♠ K and adds insult to injury by ruffing the club return to set the "laydown" game 200 points. Incidentally, West's winning the first trick with the ♡ A couldn't lose a trick. It stood only to gain, for West couldn't be prevented from winning two trumps tricks in any event.

(N-S 60 part score)
Vulnerable: Both
Dealer: E

```
               ♠  5 4 2
               ♡  10 7 5
               ◇  Q 8 3 2
               ♣  Q J 3

♠ A Q                        ♠  9 8 3
♡ 6 4 3         N            ♡  A K Q 9 8
◇ 7 5       W       E        ◇  J 6
♣ 10 9 8 7 6 2    S          ♣  K 5 4

               ♠  K J 10 7 6
               ♡  J 2
               ◇  A K 10 9 4
               ♣  A
```

Here is a hand that was played more than twenty-five years ago and remains one of the greatest defensive brilliancies I have ever come across. It was played by the late Walter Wyman and is such a stroke of genius that I would admire it almost as much if it had only been dreamed up by him and never actually been played.

The challenge begins with the opening lead, so sit yourself down in the West chair and start your imagination working.

The bidding:

EAST	SOUTH	WEST	NORTH
1♡	1♠	2♣	Pass
Pass	2◇	Pass	Pass
2♡	3◇	Pass	Pass
Pass			

Opening lead: ?

an unbeatable stroke of genius   61.

Keep in mind the North-South part score of 60, which affected the bidding and gave West considerable information to consider.

With a vulnerable South bidding unassisted to the three level, and bidding two suits, it seemed to Walter Wyman that East would be unable to deliver three defensive tricks. That being the case, West's ♠ A Q would not be enough to defeat the 3 ◇ contract. Where might another trick come from? Do you see a hope? You will have to trick the declarer, of course.

West hit upon the Machiavellian opening of the ♠ A. Then he put his partner in by leading to the ♡ Q. East, of course, assumed that his partner would ruff a spade return. So did South, who finessed the ♠ 10. Wyman

produced the ♠ Q, then put partner in with a second heart. This time when the spade came back, West ruffed for the setting trick.

Of course, if West had led a heart originally and East had shifted to a spade at once, West could have taken his ♠ A Q, then put East back in for a spade ruff. But East's natural play would be to cash one more heart, at least, and then, since partner had bid the suit, to shift to a club — possibly the ♣ K. East could hardly be expected to realize the need for an immediate spade return without West's dramatic lead of the ♠ A to guide him.

It is equally true that South could have triumphed by putting the ♠ K on the second lead of that suit. But who would dream of making such a play?

Vulnerable: None
Dealer: S

	♠ A Q J 2
	♡ Q 9 8 3
	◇ 9 8 7 6
	♣ J

♠ 10 9 8 7	**N**	♠ 6 5 3
♡ A 7 6 4	**W** **E**	♡ K 5
◇ J	**S**	◇ K 4 3 2
♣ A Q 8 7		♣ 10 5 4 2

	♠ K 4
	♡ J 10 2
	◇ A Q 10 5
	♣ K 9 6 3

Certain rules for correct play are ordinarily so dependable they may be regarded as having been brought down from Mt. Sinai in the hoary age of whist, the game that was the grandfather of contract bridge. But there is no rule so inviolable as to serve as an adequate substitute for thinking, and if West is to defeat South's optimistic 3NT contract in this deal, he is going to have to do some thinking.

Sit in West's seat, knowing that declarer has won the first trick with the ♠ K and led the ♡ J, and study the dummy for clues to a successful defense. What are your chances?

The bidding:

SOUTH	WEST	NORTH	EAST
1♣	Pass	1♠	Pass
1NT	Pass	2♡	Pass
2NT	Pass	3NT	Pass
Pass	Pass		

Opening lead: ♠ 10

62. time to break a few commandments

Since South's club strength is limited to the ♣ K, and he has affirmed control of the diamond suit by twice rebidding in notrump, you should be able to visualize the only chance you have to defeat his contract, especially as he has been kind enough to let you know who has the ♡ J. If you let him add a couple of heart tricks to the four he is known to have ready-made in spades, he'll need only three tricks in the minor suits. There is grave danger that he'll be able to win these in the diamond suit alone, and his Achilles' heel, if he has one, stands revealed as the club suit.

Have you reasoned things out thus far? Can you trust your partner to win the ♡ K — assuming he has it — and shift to clubs? And even if he does, will that stop declarer from making nine tricks?

If you've been thinking about what must be rather than about such rules as second-hand low and never lead away from an AQ combination, you've not only seen a

glimmer of hope about your prospects of winning five tricks, you've come up with the way to do something about strengthening the glimmer to a ray if not a beam. The hope is that partner has not only the ♡ K but also the ♣ 10 or the ♣ 9.

The winning defense is to bounce up with the ♡ A and lead the ♣ Q! South gets a present of a trick with the ♣ K, but it turns out to be a Greek gift when he leads another heart. East wins with the ♡ K and returns the ♣ 10 which holds the trick. (Actually, if East started with ♣9xx, it would be good enough.) You win three clubs and two hearts to stop the game.

Notice that leading a low club instead of ♣ Q wouldn't do the job. North's ♣ J wins and when East comes in with the ♡ K to lead the ♣ 10, South covers with the ♣ K. His ♣ 9 remains as a fourth-round stopper and although you've shifted to the right suit, you haven't found the right card!

Vulnerable: None
Dealer: S

```
                      ♠  7 5 4
                      ♡  9 8 6 4 2
                      ◇  A 10
                      ♣  7 6 4
♠  Q 10 6                              ♠  8 3 2
♡  J 5            N                    ♡  K 10 7 3
◇  7 4 3     W         E               ◇  J 9 6 5 2
♣  10 9 8 5 2         S                ♣  3
                      ♠  A K J 9
                      ♡  A Q
                      ◇  K Q 8
                      ♣  A K Q J
```

North-South were showing exact point holdings on strong balanced hands in this way:

2♣ followed by 2NT rebid = 23–24 HCP
3NT opening   = 25–26 HCP
2♣ followed by 3NT rebid = 27–28 HCP
2♣ followed by 4NT rebid = 29–30 HCP

In this way North could count at least 33 HCP in the combined hands, so he bid 6NT.

The opponents having reached 6NT, you, as West, open the ♣ 10. South wins the ♣ J, then cashes the ♣ A, and ♣ K, East discarding the ◇ 2 and ◇ 5.

South next cashes the ♠ A and ♠ K. What would you say are your chances of setting 6NT?

The bidding:

SOUTH	WEST	NORTH	EAST
2♣	Pass	2◇	Pass
4NT	Pass	6NT	Pass
Pass	Pass		

Opening lead: ♣ 10

helping the opponents to lose   63.

Sitting in West's chair, you know quite a bit about South's hand. After a negative response from North, South has barged into 4NT showing 29–30 points. Declarer's distribution is 4–3–2–4 or 4–2–3–4, but it is much more likely to be the latter or South would have tried to establish the hearts rather than the spades. Either he has the ♡ K and needs a diamond finesse or he has three solid diamond tricks and needs a heart finesse.

You will have to be sorting all this out while declarer is doing his own thinking, because unless the declarer is either cold for his contract or has no chance to make it, West is going to need to make a startling play and do it without giving away the show.

It is becoming reasonably clear that South has played the ♠ A K in hopes of dropping the Q or 10. Therefore, he probably began with the ♠ A K J 9 or he would have tried a spade finesse. If you drop the ♠ 10, South knows he can set up a spade trick by force even if the suit fails to split. Then he can use the ◇ A as an entry to take whatever finesse he needs in either red suit — a finesse that you know is going to win.

How can you prevent this? By provoking a finesse that will fail. You drop the ♠ Q under his ♠ K. This "impossible" play was actually made against a declarer who took so long to solve his problem, he gave West time to recognize what he must do.

Of course declarer used the only entry to dummy to take the "marked" finesse against East for the ♠ 10. Equally, of course, South was set.

Was dropping the ♠ Q dangerous? Not when South was marked with only a four-card spade suit. With only three tricks in the suit, South would need to use dummy's ◇ A in order to take the winning heart finesse.

Vulnerable: Both
Dealer: E

```
              ♠  J
              ♡  Q 7 6 3
              ◇  9 8 6 5
              ♣  J 6 4 2

♠  9 4 3                      ♠  A Q 8 7
♡  5              N           ♡  A K 10 9 4
◇  Q 10 4 3 2   W   E         ◇  A 7
♣  K 10 8 5       S           ♣  9 3

              ♠  K 10 6 5 2
              ♡  J 8 2
              ◇  K J
              ♣  A Q 7
```

The bidding:

EAST	SOUTH	WEST	NORTH
1♣	Pass	1◇	Pass
1♡	1♠	Dbl.	Pass
Pass	Pass		

Opening lead: ♡ 5

Do you trust your partner to obey your commands in the bidding? Well then, do you trust your partner when he *disobeys*?

Analysis of your partner's reasons for disregarding your wishes is the basis of the remarkable defense conducted by Benito Garozzo, West, playing with Giorgio Belladonna. East's Precision 1♣ opening was artificial, showing 16 HCP, and 1◇ was negative. South stayed out until he discovered that West was weak and that East's suit was hearts. Then he ventured to test the hot water with a spade overcall. West's double was negative: for a takeout in the minor suits. But East chose to disregard this and to defend 1♠ doubled. So assume the West seat and conduct the defense with him.

East won the ♡K and switched to the ♣9, ducked to West's ♣K. A club return was won with South's ♣A and a spade was led to the ♠J and partner's ♠Q. Next came ♡A, heart ruff with the ♠4, and a club ruff with the ♠7, South dropping the ♣Q.

64. the case of the winning discard...and why you made it

South spoiled your fun by ruffing the fourth lead of hearts with the ♠10, shutting out your ♠9. What is the winning discard? Well, if you trust your partner and have been watching the spots you discarded the ♠9! How could you tell this was the winning play? By counting out the hand and coming up with the following end position:

```
              ♠  —
              ♡  Q
              ◇  9 8 6 5
              ♣  J

♠  9                          ♠  A 8
♡  —                          ♡  10 9
◇  Q 10 4 3                   ◇  A 7
♣  8                          ♣  —

              ♠  K 10 6 5
              ♡  —
              ◇  K J
              ♣  —
```

East converted your takeout double for penalties. To do this, he must have held four spades. He has shown up with the ♠Q (to win the ♠J), and the ♠7 to ruff the third club. What could be more logical than that he should have ♠A8, for with any other spade holding, your ♠9 would not matter!

Suppose you cling to your ♠9. South leads a low spade and you win the trick. If you lead a diamond, South makes his ◇K. If you lead a club, East ruffs with the ♠A (whereupon South discards a diamond), or he lets North hold the trick with the same result. But notice the difference when you jettison the ♠9. South leads a trump and East wins the ♠A8. Next he leads his last heart and South is forced to ruff and lead away from his ◇KJ for down 1,100. Were you satisfied with a mere 800? You let the milk of human kindness interfere with milking the hand of every drop of penalty to make a Roman holiday.

Vulnerable: None
Dealer: N

```
                    ♠ K J 6
                    ♡ 3
                    ◇ A K J 9 2
                    ♣ J 10 7 5
♠ 4                              ♠ 8 7 5 2
♡ 9 7 6 4 2          N           ♡ A Q J 10 8
◇ 8 7 5 3        W     E         ◇ 6 4
♣ A 6 3              S           ♣ K Q
                    ♠ A Q 10 9 3
                    ♡ K 5
                    ◇ Q 10
                    ♣ 9 8 4 2
```

This deal is presented as a bridge mystery. You are informed that one of the East-West defenders slipped in his defense, thus enabling South to fulfill a game contract that should have been defeated. Can you finger the errant defender and detect his error?

The bidding:

NORTH	EAST	SOUTH	WEST
1◇	1♡	1♠	2♡
2♠	Pass	4♠	Pass
Pass	Pass		

Opening lead: ♡ 4

"how can I tell my partner?"

65.

After capturing the opening lead with his ♡ A, East recognized that the defenders' sole hope of defeating South's game contract rested in the club suit. To trick two he led the ♣ K, West following with the six. To trick three he continued with the ♣ Q, West completing his echo by playing the three. It didn't matter what East played next, for the declarer had the rest of the tricks.

Of course West could have defeated the contract by overtaking the ♣ Q with his ♣ A, and returning his remaining club for East to ruff. But would there have been any justification for this play? East might well have had the ♣ K Q 9, with declarer holding the ♣ 8 4 2, in which event the defenders would be able to cash three top club tricks. Which defender committed a faux pas?

Normally, as per the "book," when one is leading from a sequence of J 10 x, Q J x x, K Q x x, etc., he leads the top card of the sequence. As a defensive convention, however, in lay-outs comparable to the one contained in this deal, one deviates by design. (For example, holding A K alone, one leads the A.) At trick two East should have led the ♣ Q. Upon winning the trick, he would continue with the ♣ K. West should now properly interpret East's abnormal plays as indicating that the latter had exactly two clubs. He would then deduce the need to overtake the ♣ K with his ace and shoot back a club for East to ruff.

Even if West were not familiar with this deviation as a conventional lead, he should nevertheless overtake the ♣ K with the ♣ A. After all, West should ask himself: "Why is my partner making this unorthodox lead?" the answer would suggest itself that East is trying to convey a message. That message must be that East has no more clubs.

Vulnerable: Both
Dealer: N

```
                    ♠ 7 6 2
                    ♡ Q 10 9 3 2
                    ◇ A K 5
                    ♣ A 4
    ♠ 8 4                           ♠ K Q 10 9 5
    ♡ K 7 6          N              ♡ A 8 4
    ◇ 9 8 3 2      W   E            ◇ 7 6
    ♣ Q 10 8 6       S              ♣ 5 3 2
                    ♠ A J 3
                    ♡ J 5
                    ◇ Q J 10 4
                    ♣ K J 9 7
```

One of the skills in bridge is to force the opponents to play the way you want them to, rather than allow them to play as they'd like.

East gave over the initiative to the declarer when he defended 3NT in this deal. The result: A lost chance to defeat the game.

Do you see how East could have given the declarer no choice but to lose the hand?

The bidding:

NORTH	EAST	SOUTH	WEST
1 ♡	1 ♠	2NT	Pass
3NT	Pass	Pass	Pass

Opening lead: ♠ 8

66. ability to quack doesn't make a duck

When East quacked 1 ♠ over the opening bid of 1 ♡, he risked being set 500 points but his overcall helped get partner off to the only lead that might have set the 3NT contract. So his was a worthwhile bid, especially as it is rare, in this day of negative doubles, to play at a doubled contract of one in a suit.

Alas, East put his ♠ Q on the first trick and thereby surrendered control of the timing to declarer. South ducked, allowing the ♠ Q to hold. When declarer won the spade continuation, it was safe for him to set up the heart suit as long as East didn't hold both the ♡ A and ♡ K. If West won the first heart trick, he would not have a spade to lead; if East won the first heart, he would have no reentry to cash the spades after he had set them up.

But notice how East can alter the timing so that South cannot make his contract. East must realize that declarer surely has three spades including the ♠ A J. East

must be prepared to surrender two tricks in the spade suit, and the only hope of defeating the contract is if West has the ♡ K. (If declarer has that card he is virtually certain to make nine tricks.) But what good will it do if partner wins a trick with the ♡ K and no longer has a spade to lead?

The winning defense is now clear. Play the ♠ 9 on the first trick, forcing South to use one of his stoppers at once or give up his second stopper entirely. Now, when declarer tackles the hearts, West wins the first lead with his ♡ K and leads his remaining spade.

It does not matter whether or not South ducks the second spade. East is able to set up three tricks in the suit while he holds the ♡ A as a reentry. South's only chance to win nine tricks is via the club finesse. When it loses, West puts partner in with the ♡ A and East-West collect 200 instead of losing the game.

Vulnerable: E-W
Dealer: S

```
              ♠ Q J 10 9 4
              ♡ 6 2
              ◇ Q 7 5
              ♣ 9 4 2

♠ 6 5                      ♠ 8 7 3
♡ A Q 8 5 4       N        ♡ 9 7 3
◇ 10 9         W     E     ◇ A J 6 2
♣ J 8 6 3         S        ♣ Q 10 5

              ♠ A K 2
              ♡ K J 10
              ◇ K 8 4 3
              ♣ A K 7
```

When contract was in its infancy, many players were of the opinion that plain, ordinary common sense was all that was required to play out a hand, or to defend, in winning fashion. They were wrong, as the passage of time and the impact of experience have demonstrated.

With the above as a clue, let's see how you, sitting East, defend against South's three no-trump contract.

The bidding:

SOUTH	WEST	NORTH	EAST
1 ◇	Pass	1 ♠	Pass
3NT	Pass	Pass	Pass

Opening lead: ♡ 5

You put up the ♡ 9 on the opening lead, and South takes the trick with the ♡ 10. The next three tricks look like this:

SOUTH	WEST	NORTH	EAST
♠ A	♠ 6	♠ 4	♠ 3
♠ K	♠ 5	♠ 9	♠ 7
◇ K	◇ 10	◇ 5	?

There is no question in your mind that declarer is trying to make an entry out of dummy's ◇ Q in order to cash the board's remaining spades. You don't know what the heart set-up is but if you take your ◇ A, you will enable him to accomplish his objective. So you let South hold the ◇ K. Now to your surprise, South produces the ♠ 2, and comes home with nine tricks.

Of course your partner then points out (as if you didn't know) that if you had taken the ◇ K with the ◇ A and returned a heart, he would have cashed four heart tricks. Based on "common sense" (or shall we say guess-work), you really would be at a loss as to whether to accept or reject South's offering of the ◇ K. But familiarity with "science" would have told you to take it.

Whenever declarer is trying to establish a suit in dummy, or is trying to create an entry for a suit that is established, your partner should give you a "count." When declarer led the ♠ K at trick two, your partner played the ♠ 6. On the next lead of the ♠ A, he followed suit with the ♠ 5. In these situations, partner plays high-low to show two or four of the suit being led. Thus South was known to still hold the ♠ 2, since if West had held the 6 5 2, he would have played the ♠ 2 on the original lead, and followed next with the ♠ 5.

And so South tried to pull the wool over your eyes with a bid of chicanery? Did he succeed?

♠ J 10 9 3
♡ A 10 4
◇ K 4
♣ K Q 7 2

♠ 2
♡ J 8 6 3
◇ J 10 9 7
♣ 9 8 5 4

N
W E
S

♠ K Q 6
♡ Q 9 7 2
◇ A Q 3 2
♣ 6 3

♠ A 8 7 5 4
♡ K 5
◇ 8 6 5
♣ A J 10

The bidding:

SOUTH	WEST	NORTH	EAST
1♠	Pass	3♠	Pass
4♠	Pass	Pass	Pass

Opening lead: ◇ J

The plan for a winning defense must frequently be set into operation early in the play. As a defender — in this case East — you should be thinking furiously all the while the declarer is studying the tabled dummy and laying his own plans.

West's opening lead of the ◇ J causes declarer some momentary study and gives you time to scheme before he decides to play dummy's ◇ 4. How are your chances?

68. getting into the act

Obviously — since you see so much stuff in your hand and dummy — opener has a minimum bid and presumably a five-card spade suit. You expect to win two diamond tricks, but, since South is marked with the ♡ K and ♣ A, in addition to the ♠ A, you see no possibility of another trick in a side suit.

Your only chance to defeat the contract lies in winning two trump tricks, but the proper play of such a suit is for declarer to lead the ♠ J through and let it ride; then, if it loses (which you can see it won't), he goes back to dummy to take another finesse. Therefore, if declarer follows the book play, he is certain to make his contract. Can you persuade him to abandon the winning play? The fact that your ♣ 3 is known to be the lowest, since North has the ♣ 2, gives you some hope.

So you overtake partner's ◇ J with your ◇ Q in order to lead the ♣ 3. You hope to convince declarer that if he

loses a first-round trump finesse into West's hand, you will be able to ruff a club return.

South overtakes his ♣ J with dummy's ♣ Q and leads the ♠ J. You play the ♠ 6, of course, and wait to see if declarer has swallowed your bait.

Declarer may see through your plot and let the ♠ J ride — as he would surely have done if you simply let partner continue leading diamonds. If so, you have lost nothing, but at least you have tried. However, if declarer elects to go up with the ♠ A, hoping to drop an honor from West or that the suit will split 2–2 (which, percentagewise, isn't far off the preferred play), your scheme will triumph. When he continues trumps, you'll win your ♠ K and ♠ Q, lay down the ◇ A and close your eyes. When you open them you see a red card on the table and a red flush on declarer's cheek. Down one.

Vulnerable: None
Dealer: S

```
                     ♠ 9 8 5 3
                     ♡ Q J 9
                     ◇ A J 10 2
                     ♣ 7 3
  ♠ 4                      N          ♠ A 7 2
  ♡ 10 7 3                            ♡ 8 6 5 4 2
  ◇ K 8 7 6 5      W       E          ◇ 4
  ♣ K Q 8 4                           ♣ A 9 6 5
                          S
                     ♠ K Q J 10 6
                     ♡ A K
                     ◇ Q 9 3
                     ♣ J 10 2
```

When a defender's opening lead is the king or queen of an unbid suit, if his partner wants him to continue playing that suit, he will signal for a continuation by playing an unnecessarily high card. Such is the basic principle. But many occasions arise where judgment supersedes principle.

As East you must find the winning defense.

The bidding:

SOUTH	WEST	NORTH	EAST
1♠	Pass	2♠	Pass
3♠	Pass	4♠	Pass
Pass	Pass		

Opening lead: ♣ K

are you too quick on the draw?

It is obvious that West possesses the ♣Q, and if East plays the ♣9, the defenders can collect two tricks in a hurry. West will certainly continue the club suit, with East's ♣A winning the trick. East would then shift to a heart, hoping that his partner could win a trick in this suit. But, on this day, East would be fighting a losing cause.

There is really no assurance — for that matter, based on the bidding — not even a decent hope that West will have a heart trick. But, more important, there is no necessity to indulge in any wishful thinking with regard to the heart suit. If South has two clubs — a much more realistic possibility than that West holds either the ♡A or ♡K — East can defeat the contract.

Far from wanting a club continuation, East wants partner to shift to a diamond. So, taking his finger off the ♣9 that would automatically signal the ♣A, East is about to play the discouraging ♣5 when he stops to think a little further. Why leave it to partner to understand that a diamond shift is essential?

So East doesn't do any signalling. He simply overtakes partner's ♣K with the ♣A and leads his ◇4 into the jaws of dummy's powerful holding in that suit. South follows as deceptively as he can with the ◇9 and West's ◇K is taken by the board's ◇A.

At trick three, when a low trump is led off dummy, East rises with his ♠A. The ♣5 is now returned to West's known ♣Q and East can hardly be in any doubt that a diamond continuation is desired. East's ruff now scores the setting trick.

The moral of my tale? Would you rather defeat a contract or win a later argument? Had East played the ♣5 on the first trick, he might reasonably complain that West should have shifted to a diamond. But West would have a better cause for complaint. "Why didn't you do it yourself, John?"

```
                    ♠  A J
                    ♡  K 9 6
                    ◇  Q J 9 5
                    ♣  Q J 10 6
   ♠  7 6 5                        ♠  K 10 4 3 2
   ♡  Q 8 4 3          N           ♡  J 5 2
   ◇  A 7 2        W       E       ◇  8 4 3
   ♣  A 5 4            S           ♣  7 2
                    ♠  Q 9 8
                    ♡  A 10 7
                    ◇  K 10 6
                    ♣  K 9 8 3
```

Often in pair tournaments, and frequently in rubber bridge as well, giving declarer an extra trick by your opening lead can be expensive. In such cases leading a short suit may prove the most effective defense. West's ♠ 7 hit East's lone best hope of winning some tricks for the defenders.

You are invited to take East's chair and find the winning defense when dummy's ♠ J is played to the first trick.

The bidding:

NORTH	EAST	SOUTH	WEST
1♣	Pass	2NT	Pass
3NT	Pass	Pass	Pass

Opening lead: ♠ 7

70. sorry pard . . . I pulled the wrong card!

I have often suspected that when this defensive gem was first discovered it was the result of an accident. If so, it was a most effective one.

What do you return after you have won the first trick with your ♠ K? The answer is that it doesn't really matter. You have — as they say in the trade — already blown the duke. No shift is going to do any good, even if you shift to West's longest suit, hearts. Declarer is going to win three clubs, three diamonds, a couple of spades and at least two hearts. The only tricks the defense can garner are your ♠ K and partner's two aces.

Nor does it help if you continue spades. Declarer will have to let partner in twice with his ♣ A and ◇ A, but the second time he gets in he will not have another spade to lead.

What can East do about it? He can "accidentally"

play the ♠ 10 under the ♠ J! Can this play be anything but an accident? Indeed, yes. South can hardly have bid 2NT with just the ♠ 65. So, partner's lead must be top of nothing, yet he cannot have more than three spades because there are only two lower ones missing. You have no entry, so your only hope is that partner has two. But for this to avail you have to leave him a card to put you in with. This can only be a third spade. So you let dummy win the first trick with the ♠ J and, since your others are so low, you might as well signal with the ♠ 10.

Note the difference when you duck that first spade. Declarer still wins two spade tricks — but you have made him take the first and second and left yourself with the card to win the third. Three spade tricks, plus partner's two aces are enough to stop 3NT.

Vulnerable: N-S
Dealer: N

```
                 ♠ 7 5
                 ♡ 8 3
                 ◇ A Q 10 9 3
                 ♣ K Q J 4
♠ 8 4                        ♠ K 6 3
♡ A K 7 5 2        N         ♡ Q J 9
◇ 6 4 2        W     E       ◇ 7 5
♣ 7 5 3            S         ♣ A 10 8 6 2
                 ♠ A Q J 10 9 2
                 ♡ 10 6 4
                 ◇ K J 8
                 ♣ 9
```

Here is a chance for you to demonstrate your defensive ability. When the deal arose in actual competition, the East defender flubbed his opportunity. Let's see if you can meet the challenge.

West opens the ♡ K, and you, sitting East, are in the captain's seat. What is your plan of defense?

The bidding:

NORTH	EAST	SOUTH	WEST
1◇	Pass	1♠	Pass
2♣	Pass	4♠	Pass
Pass	Pass		

Opening lead: ♡ K

when you know, don't let partner guess 71.

When the deal was actually played, East followed with the ♡ 9 on West's ♡ K and played the ♡ J on West's ♡ A. At trick three West shifted to a diamond, dummy's ◇ 9 winning the trick. Declarer successfully finessed the ♠ 9, after which the ◇ J was led and overtaken by the ◇ Q. Next came another spade finesse, followed by the ace, felling East's ♠ K. Declarer ended up taking 11 tricks — six trumps and five diamonds. East then asked his partner why he hadn't continued hearts. "You didn't ask me to," West replied, "so I thought you wanted a shift."

After partner leads the ♡ K and the dummy comes into view, it looks like your side has two heart winners and one club. It appears as though you will need to win a trick with your trump king if the contract is to be set. Unhappily, you know that your ♠ K is under the gun. If declarer is left to his own resources, he will take two finesses against your king, and thus avoid the loss of a trump trick (surely, on the bidding, declarer has an otherwise solid six- or seven-card trump suit). How can you promote your trump king into a winner?

On partner's ♡ K you play the ♡ Q. This is a conventional defensive play: whenever one plays the queen on partner's king, he is commanding partner to underlead his ace. At trick two, West obediently leads the ♡ 5, which you capture with the ♡ J. For your third trick you cash the ♣ A. Then you come back with the ♡ 9, which is covered by South's ♡ 10 and West's ♡ K. Declarer has no choice but to ruff the trick in dummy.

He next leads the board's remaining trump and finesses against your ♠ K. He lays down the ♠ A, hoping that you were dealt the ♠ K with only one other spade. You weren't — and in time your ♠ K takes the setting trick.

Vulnerable: None
Dealer: N

```
              ♠ 10 6
              ♡ A 5
              ◇ A Q 8 6 5 4
              ♣ J 7 3

♠ A K J 9 7 5          N          ♠ Q 8 4 2
♡ 9 6 4 2                         ♡ Q 8 3
◇ J 9          W    E             ◇ 3 2
♣ 4                 S             ♣ A 8 6 5

              ♠ 3
              ♡ K J 10 7
              ◇ K 10 7
              ♣ K Q 10 9 2
```

It is good policy for a defender with a sure trump trick not to rush to spend it too soon. In this deal, for example, after South had used his ♣ 2 to ruff West's continuation of the ♠ A, East wisely refused to win either the lead of South's ♣ K, on which West followed with the ♣ 4, or his follow-up of the ♣ 10, on which West discarded ♠ 5.

South shifted to the ◇ 10, covered by the ◇ J and won by North's ◇ Q. The next trick comprised the ◇ A, 3, 7, and 9 and East had to choose his best play when dummy led the ◇ 4. Take over East's seat.

The bidding:

NORTH	EAST	SOUTH	WEST
1 ◇	Pass	2 ♣	2 ♠
Pass	Pass	3 ♡	Pass
4 ♣	Pass	5 ♣	Pass
Pass	Pass		

Opening lead: ♠ K

72. don't be blinded by a pinch of dust

From time to time, our description of your problem may include a pinch of dust, but that is fair enough since your opponents will be doing their best to mislead you at every opportunity.

Were you wary of handing declarer his contract by ruffing the third diamond? If you trumped high, the ♣ J and the ♡ A would both remain as entries to dummy and declarer would have no trouble winning his game. If you trumped low and were overruffed, South would leave you with your ♣ A and cross to dummy's ♡ A, continuing with good diamonds. Whenever you chose to spend your ♣ A, he would then be in a position to get to dummy with the ♣ J and run the remainder of the diamond suit.

Then did you discard a low heart or a low spade? It does not matter. You have fallen victim to the pinch of dust. South produces the missing ◇ K, crosses to dummy's ♡ A and runs good diamonds. Once again, you are on the prongs of Morton's fork. If you ruff low, South overruffs, cashes the ♡ K, ruffs a heart and continues leading good diamonds. Your ♣ A is your only trick.

How could you have known that it was right to ruff that third diamond lead? Go back to the bidding and you will see it clearly enough. South is known to have begun with five clubs and only one spade. If he did not have a third diamond, he must have started with five hearts, surely to at least the king. But in that event, he would have responded 1 ♡ originally, not 2 ♣, bidding the higher of two suits of equal length.

Your holdup of the ♣ A for two rounds has forced him to fall back upon guile because if he continued trumps, you would win the third round and revert to spades, forcing out his last trump and leaving your ♣ 8 as the setting trick.

Vulnerable: None
Dealer: S

```
                  ♠ 9 5 2
                  ♡ K J
                  ◇ A Q J 7 4
                  ♣ J 3 2

♠ Q 10 8 4                      ♠ K J 6 3
♡ 5 4           N               ♡ A Q 2
◇ 10 9 3 2    W   E             ◇ 6 5
♣ 8 7 6          S             ♣ Q 10 9 4

                  ♠ A 7
                  ♡ 10 9 8 7 6 3
                  ◇ K 8
                  ♣ A K 5
```

Defending as East you should break a rule on the very first trick. It is most unlikely your partner has underled the ♠A, and you are anxious to read declarer's hand in order to determine the best defense.

So you scrap the first word in the usually valid advice, "Never finesse against your partner," and put in the ♠J. South takes the ♠A and leads to the ♡J. You are in with the ♡Q and have a problem: how are you going to defeat the 4♡ contract?

The bidding:

SOUTH	WEST	NORTH	EAST
1♡	Pass	2◇	Pass
2♡	Pass	3♡	Pass
4♡	Pass	Pass	Pass

Opening lead: ♠ 4

more advice from "The Light Brigade"

Tennyson's poem is about the gallant charge at Balaclava, not about bridge. But because I have always liked the poem, I'm using it as a veiled clue to the successful defense of this deal.

You have established by your first play that partner has the ♠Q. You cash the ♠K and it lives. It is not impossible that partner has led from a three-card suit, but it seems likely that if South held two spade losers, he'd have played for the diamonds to furnish a discard or two before tackling trumps. So you decide declarer does not have another spade, and with dummy's diamond holding in plain view, it is obvious that the setting trick can come only from clubs. But before tackling that suit you hark back to the bidding and realize that South simply would not have gone on to game on such a shabby suit unless he has the ♣AK. So, even if South doesn't let a shift to the ♣4 ride to dummy's ♣J, he'll still have time to get a

discard or two on dummy's diamonds.

Recapping South's hand, it shapes up as six hearts (from his rebids) and most probably two spades. Also, unless he has at least three clubs you are unlikely to beat him. But that leaves him with only two diamonds at most. (He could have a singleton diamond and four clubs.) Does this suggest the way you can neutralize the diamond suit? Lead one immediately!

You lead a diamond and South takes the ◇K. He leads another trump and you capture the ♡K with your ♡A. Back comes another diamond "into the jaws of death" and it is dummy that is killed. South has to try to get a discard on a third round of diamonds but you ruff with your now far from innocuous ♡2 and declarer is down to the vain hope that the ♣Q will fall in two rounds. It doesn't and if you successfully met this challenge, I heartily congratulate you.

Vulnerable: N-S
Dealer: S

```
                    ♠ A 9 7
                    ♡ Q 5 3
                    ◇ K Q J 6 5 4
                    ♣ J

♠ 6 5 4                              ♠ K 3
♡ K 9 6 4          N                 ♡ 10 7 2
◇ 3            W         E           ◇ A 9 7 2
♣ 9 8 7 5 3        S                 ♣ Q 10 6 4

                    ♠ Q J 10 8 2
                    ♡ A J 8
                    ◇ 10 8
                    ♣ A K 2
```

In playing card peerage a count can be more important than a king or a queen.

A count of the unseen cards; a count of the tricks available to your side; a count of the missing points around the table — these can be the determining factors between winning and losing.

You, East, can be sure that your partner's ◇ 3 is a singleton, so you can also be sure to get a diamond ruff and the ♠ K. If West has an ace, the contract is defeated. But what if he doesn't?

The bidding:

SOUTH	WEST	NORTH	EAST
1 ♠	Pass	2 ◇	Pass
2NT	Pass	3 ♠	Pass
4 ♠	Pass	Pass	Pass

Opening lead: ◇ 3

74. find the setting trick

If you are like the ordinary bridge player, you have already given your partner a diamond ruff at the second trick before you have thought about the necessity of finding a fourth trick to set the contract. Slow up a bit, and you'll collect more profits.

You have a second entry in the presence of the ♠ K. But declarer is marked with only two diamonds and he will probably be able to ruff a third diamond lead high enough to shut your partner out. Even if he began with a five-card suit headed by the ♠ J 10, he will simply play ace and another spade and your honors will drop together. So you have to find your fourth trick before you find your second.

If partner has the ♡ A or the ♣ A, his trick will need no establishing. But what if he holds the ♡ K? When you give him a diamond ruff, he won't be able to lead the suit from his side of the table without giving up a trick.

If you are counting, you know that partner probably has three trumps, so it won't do him any harm to postpone that diamond ruff. Instead, play a heart. It doesn't matter whether declarer finesses or not. He may go up with the ♡ A and gamble everything on the spade finesse. When you get in with the ♠ K, you give your partner a diamond ruff. If he has the ♡ K, he'll cash it for the setting trick.

HELPFUL HINT: Before rushing to grab a trick, count how many you'll need. When one trick won't do, look for a way to win two.

Vulnerable: N-S
Dealer: S

```
                    ♠ K 8 3
                    ♡ 9 5
                    ◇ Q J 10 4
                    ♣ K J 6 3
♠ 10 6 5                         ♠ Q J 9 2
♡ A 10 8 6          N            ♡ J 7 4 3 2
◇ K 7 2        W         E       ◇ 8
♣ Q 10 9            S            ♣ 7 5 4
                    ♠ A 7 4
                    ♡ K Q
                    ◇ A 9 6 5 3
                    ♣ A 8 2
```

The bidding:

SOUTH	WEST	NORTH	EAST
1NT	Pass	3NT	Pass
Pass	Pass		

Opening lead: ♡ 6

Rules can be valuable guides to successful play, but they are not a substitute for thinking. Such shibboleths, as "Always return your partner's suit," and "Second hand low," must always give way to still another generality: "Circumstances alter cases."

Apparently, East had little to do about the result of this deal and yet what he did was to decide the result. Put yourself in his chair and plan your defense when partner opens the ♡ 6.

East followed the rule

East was happy that partner's lead had found his longest suit, but South was far less so. Apparently the 3NT contract was going to depend upon the diamond finesse.

Perhaps if declarer had faced more of a problem, East would have seen that he had one, too. But East played third-hand high, the ♡ J, and the defense collapsed. The diamond finesse lost, but West could run only three heart tricks and the setting trick — the fifth heart — languished in East's hand.

The Rule of 11 told East that declarer had two cards higher than the ♡ 6. So East played the ♡ J to prevent declarer from winning two tricks in hearts with ♡ A 10 or ♡ A 8. Also, because the "rule" is "third-hand high." But, supposing that declarer could win two heart tricks instead of one, playing the ♡ J on the first trick could not help. West would then need two outside tricks to defeat the contract. And if West had two entries, the

defenders could collect three heart tricks, provided East hung onto ♡ J.

East could tell just by looking at his hand and the dummy that unless he clung to his ♡ J, there would be no way to collect more than three heart tricks. Any other card would be better — the ♡ 7 or any card that would express enthusiasm without sacrificing the only entry that could possibly bring home the fifth heart.

As the cards lay, South would have to win the trick with his ♡ Q. When the finesse for the ◇ K lost West could be in no doubt that a heart continuation was desired. The appearance of the dummy and East's ♡ 7 should put him on the right track. His ♡ A would fell the ♡ K, the ♡ 10 would be allowed to hold, but East would then be able to overtake the ♡ 8 with the ♡ J and cash the setting trick.

Vulnerable: E-W
Dealer: S

```
                    ♠ 9 6
                    ♡ 8 6 5 2
                    ♢ 9 5 3
                    ♣ K Q J 10
  ♠ 5 3 2                        ♠ A K Q 10 7
  ♡ 7              N             ♡ 10 4 3
  ♢ Q 7 6 2    W     E           ♢ J 10 8
  ♣ 9 8 6 5 4      S             ♣ A 2
                    ♠ J 8 4
                    ♡ A K Q J 9
                    ♢ A K 4
                    ♣ 7 3
```

When this deal was played, the East defender produced an excellent play to ultimately defeat South's game contract. You are invited to equal it. After capturing tricks one and two with the ♠ Q and ♠ A, what is your play to trick three?

The bidding:

SOUTH	WEST	NORTH	EAST
1 ♡	Pass	2 ♡	2 ♠
4 ♡	Pass	Pass	Pass

Opening lead: ♠ 5

76. what must South hold?

The instinctive play, I think, would be to lead the ◇ J, and hope that your partner has the ◇ K. If that is East's choice, South's problems are over. He wins the the trick with the ◇ A, draws trumps in three rounds, and leads a club. East declines to win this lead, but is compelled to take the second club. Now he leads another diamond. But South has the ◇ K. Declarer reaches dummy by ruffing his ♠ J, and discards his remaining diamond on the ♣ J.

Before playing to the third trick, however, East stopped to reconstruct declarer's probable hand. South still had the ♠ J because West had led the ♠ 5 and followed with the ♠ 3 on the second trick. Had West held either ♠ J53, or J532 he would have led the lowest card, not the ♠ 5. With nothing better than the ♠ J in either black suit, South must have solid trumps and the ◇ AK to justify his jump to game, so any hope that partner has better than the ◇ Q must be in vain. Now what

was South's exact distribution? It was virtually impossible that he had leaped all the way to game after a mere single raise if he held three losers in both the black suits. Then, too, if South had three or more clubs, the contract could not be defeated for his hand must be at least ♠ J84 ♡ AKQ97 ◇ AK ♣ 987. South would merely draw trumps, give up the ♣ A, and ruff his ♠ J in dummy.

Then what holding must South have that might allow the contract to be set? This is so often the question a defender must ask himself if the winning defense is to be found. It enabled East to assume exactly what South held: only two clubs and ◇ AKx. "Seeing" this hand in his mind's eye, East came up with the winning defense. He led the ♠ K and forced declarer to use his reentry to dummy before he could establish the club suit.

After that, it was only necessary for East to duck one round of clubs and dummy was dead. Eventually, South had to concede a diamond as the setting trick.

Vulnerable: None
Dealer: S

```
                    ♠  5 3 2
                    ♡  K J 6
                    ◇  K Q 6 5
                    ♣  7 5 2
  ♠  A K Q 10              N          ♠  J 4
  ♡  5 4 3            W         E     ♡  10 9 8 2
  ◇  J 9 8                 S          ◇  7 4 3 2
  ♣  9 6 4                            ♣  Q J 10
                    ♠  9 8 7 6
                    ♡  A Q 7
                    ◇  A 10
                    ♣  A K 8 3
```

Every once in a while, you are entitled to expect an "easy" one. Or is this one so very easy?

West rattled off the first four spade tricks with his ♠ A K Q 10. South follows to all of them. East's problem is how to handle the discarding.

The bidding:

SOUTH	WEST	NORTH	EAST
1 NT	Pass	2NT	Pass
3NT	Pass	Pass	Pass

Opening lead: ♠ Q

what you see is what you get

Your opponents are playing the customary strong no-trump — 16–18 high card points, which they sometimes shade to 15–17. When partner shows up with the top spades, you have a pretty good count on South's hand, as far as his high cards are concerned.

He has bid the game over North's encouraging but by no means forcing raise to 2 NT, so you assume that he holds something more than a minimum. Taking into account the high cards you can see in your hand and the dummy, you can be sure that he must hold at least the ◇ A, the ♡ A Q and the ♣ A K. Eight tricks on top. Then where is the setting trick coming from?

Despite your solid holding in hearts, you know that you won't take a trick in that suit. If South has more than three cards in the suit, he is going to take tricks with his four top honors. So you discard two hearts on the spades, and dummy lets go the ♣ 2. West — with an "I've-done-my-share" look at you — neatly packs his four tricks into your book and shifts to the ♡ 5.

Which is all very well, but when South cashes his three good hearts (to all of which partner follows), you are now forced to make another discard. Obviously you can't part with one of your three powerful clubs, so you throw your ◇ 2. Or do you?

It isn't "obvious" that you cannot spare a club. In fact, your only hope is that partner has the ♣ 9, for you can see that he cannot hold more than three diamonds and that if you unguard your precious ◇ 7, dummy's ◇ 6 will surely score the ninth trick.

If you threw the ♣ 10, your faith is rewarded. When declarer cashes his three top diamonds, it turns out that West began with ◇ J 9 8. Your ◇ 7 holds mastery over dummy's ◇ 6. And, as a reward for your faith, partner has the twice-guarded ♣ 9 to win the setting trick.

Vulnerable: E-W
Dealer: S

```
                    ♠ 7 4
                    ♡ K 10
                    ◇ K J 6 5 4
                    ♣ A 7 3 2
 ♠ 9 8                           ♠ A 5
 ♡ J 8 7 3          N            ♡ A Q 6 2
 ◇ Q 2          W       E        ◇ 10 9 7 3
 ♣ J 10 6 5 4       S            ♣ K Q 8
                    ♠ K Q J 10 6 3 2
                    ♡ 9 5 4
                    ◇ A 8
                    ♣ 9
```

The bidding:

SOUTH	WEST	NORTH	EAST
4 ♠	Pass	Pass	Pass

Opening lead: ♡ 3

Experts often astonish less accomplished players by calling off the unseen hands after only a few plays.

Sometimes, however, it is necessary to perform this bit of virtuosity at the very first trick. It helps when you know an opponent is orthodox in his conservatism.

You are challenged to solve East's problem after dummy's ♡ K is played on the first trick and you win the trick with your ♡ A. How are you going to get the four tricks you will need to defeat the contract?

78. putting on your thinking cap

What do know from the bidding? According to the Rule of 2 and 3, which you know is religiously followed by this declarer, he must be able to win within three tricks of his bid when not vulnerable. Therefore, he needs either eight spades solid but for your ♠ A, or seven spades with an outside trick.

How much can you tell from the first trick? West has led from a four-card suit and both his lead of a low card (indicating something in the suit), and South's play of dummy's ♡ K suggest that partner has the ♡ J, so South probably began with three small hearts.

Assuming declarer holds eight spades, he won't have an outside trick and there'll be no problem about your partner getting his ◇ A or your winning a club trick. Your concern, therefore, is that South may hold only seven spades with the doubleton ◇ A as his outside trick. It will then be necessary that you get all three of your heart tricks to defeat the contract. But you can't do that in a hurry because dummy threatens to ruff the third round of hearts.

An obvious solution is to remove dummy's trumps by leading ♠ A and ♠ 5. But if you do that, it will be easy for declarer to win three diamonds and a club in addition to six spade tricks.

The answer? Lead your ♠ 5. If your partner doesn't have the ◇ A, he must have two trumps and South won't be able to get any quick discards on the diamonds because partner will be able to ruff the third round.

Try this play against any combination except declarer's holding all the missing spades higher than the ♠ 7 with ♡ 9 5 4 ◇ A x x ♣ — as his outside distribution. Then he'd be able to win the spade in dummy and take an immediate heart discard on the ♣ A. But then, if West held a singleton diamond, would he not have opened it in preference to leading from a measly four hearts to the ♡ J?

Vulnerable: N-S
Dealer: S

```
                      ♠ A 5
                      ♡ Q 10
                      ◇ 6 5 3 2
                      ♣ K J 7 6 5
♠ 10 8 7 3 2                        ♠ K J 6
♡ 9 5 2            N                ♡ 8 7 6 4 3
◇ A J 9 7      W       E            ◇ Q 10
♣ 3               S                 ♣ Q 10 2
                      ♠ Q 9 4
                      ♡ A K J
                      ◇ K 8 4
                      ♣ A 9 8 4
```

Players who open fourth best both receive and give considerable information. But sometimes the information conveyed is not enough to make your future action clear. East found himself in this kind of position when partner opened the ♠ 3 and declarer played the ♠ 5 from dummy.

Knowing that the opponents play 16–18 point notrump openings, and that your partner leads fourth highest, how will you, East, defend this deal so as to discover the necessary road to the five tricks you will need to defeat the contract?

The bidding:

SOUTH	WEST	NORTH	EAST
1 NT	Pass	3NT	Pass
Pass	Pass		

Opening lead: ♠ 3

point of information: how to find a winning way 79.

Your partner's lead of the ♠ 3 tells you that declarer must have at least three spades because if partner has the only lower card, the ♠ 2, he will still have only a five-card suit. So you would like to know two things: Does partner have five spades, and, if so, do they include the ♠ Q? If declarer has the ♠ Q, he is sure of winning at least two spade tricks; if he tackles the clubs, he is going to score four tricks in that suit, assuming that he has the ♣ A, and the minimum of 10 points he must hold in the red suits will probably be enough to give him the three additional tricks he will need for his contract.

One thing you can find out at once is the location of the ♠ Q, though it may cost you a trick to do so. If you go up with the ♠ K and return the ♠ J, you will soon enough learn whether partner has a fifth spade. You *might*—if partner is experienced enough—instead ascertain that he does *not* have the ♠ Q. Assuming that he holds the ♠ 10 as his highest card, he should drop this under your ♠ J in order to warn you that the ♠ Q is missing. (Obviously, if

he held the ♠ Q 10, he could afford to signal with the higher card, so the ♠ 10 would warn you to shift.)

Simpler, however, is to play the ♠ J on the first trick. If South has the ♠ Q, he will win it. However, if your ♠ J wins, you will know that partner has at least four to the ♠ Q and you should continue the suit, unblocking by returning your ♠ K to the ♠ A in the hope that partner will be able to show you that he has five—and that by retaining your ♠ 6 you can later put him in to run three more spades.

As the cards lie, South will win the first trick with the ♠ Q. He'll lay down the ♣ A and try to establish the club suit. To do this, he must let you win a trick with the ♣ Q. But now you know that it is futile to continue spades and you shift to the ◇ Q as your only hope. The gods and the cards are kind. West has the exact holding necessary to win four fast diamond tricks whether or not South covers the ◇ Q with his ◇ K. You have broken a rule—third hand high. But you have also broken a contract.

```
                    ♠ A 9
                    ♡ Q 10 7 4
                    ◇ A K J 6 5
                    ♣ Q 3

♠ K J 6 5 4              N              ♠ 8 3 2
♡ 9 8                              ♡ K J 6 3
◇ 7 3 2           W       E        ◇ Q 10 9 4
♣ A 8 5                S              ♣ 7 2

                    ♠ Q 10 7
                    ♡ A 5 2
                    ◇ 8
                    ♣ K J 10 9 6 4
```

Hardly anything is more irritating than to have partner turn a deaf ear to the bidding. So East was pleased that West had not opened the spade suit, for which declarer was so obviously prepared. Instead, the lead was the ♡ 9 covered by the ♡ 10 and ♡ J, with South dropping the ♡ 5.

You are challenged to take over East's chair and continue the defense. And be warned, your task is *not* easy.

Watch out for booby traps.

There's something odd about your having won the first trick with the ♡ J. Before you turn this trick over, study it again.

The bidding:

NORTH	EAST	SOUTH	WEST
1◇	Pass	2♣	Pass
2♡	Pass	2NT	Pass
3NT	Pass	Pass	Pass

Opening lead: ♡ 9

80. you have to wonder: "Why?"

Can partner have the ♡ A? If so, why did he lead the ♡ 9 rather than a lower one? It doesn't seem likely he'd do that, so you surmise that South has the top heart. Then "Why?" — the essential question — "Why did he let me hold the first trick?" Especially as he has just played the ♡ 5 and must know there's a good chance he can win three heart tricks if he uses the ♡ A to take your ♡ J.

South must be hoping to win several tricks in clubs, but apparently his suit isn't solid. You begin to get the idea that he does not have a sure reentry other than the ♡ A and he'd like to hold on to it. Partner almost surely has the ♠ K and either the ♣ A or a well guarded ♣ K, with which he can hold off to prevent the establishment of the club suit.

You still haven't turned the first trick over. If South had started with ♡ A 8 5, he could take your ♡ J and still be sure of a reentry. So West must have the ♡ 8. If you've followed this line of reasoning thus far, you have done

well. But if you lead back a small heart, expecting the ♡ A to drop, you've underestimated declarer. He produces the ♡ 2, wins the trick in dummy and proceeds to establish the clubs. West has ♣ A 8 5, but holding off will do no good.

Back to the second trick. The only way to be sure you force out the ♡ A is to continue with the ♡ K! Yes, you've given South an extra trick in hearts. But you've saved five tricks in clubs. Whether declarer tries for the game-going tricks in spades or diamonds he is now headed for defeat. You are certain to have won at least a heart and a club with three more tricks sure to come from the spade and diamond suits.

Declarer may try various ways to develop nine tricks, but all of them can be countered successfully if West holds up the ♣ A until the second round of the suit.

After that, wriggle as he may, if the defense is alert the declarer must end up at least one trick short.

Vulnerable: E-W
Dealer: N

```
                 ♠ 6 3
                 ♡ —
                 ◇ A Q 10 7 6
                 ♣ A K Q 8 6 5

♠ 9 7                        ♠ J 10 5
♡ J 7 5          N           ♡ K Q 10 9 6 4 2
◇ K 9 8 4 2   W     E        ◇ —
♣ J 9 7          S           ♣ 10 4 3

                 ♠ A K Q 8 4 2
                 ♡ A 8 3
                 ◇ J 5 3
                 ♣ 2
```

The bidding:

NORTH	EAST	SOUTH	WEST
1♣	2♡	2♠	Pass
3◇	Pass	3♡	Pass
4◇	Dbl.	4♠	Pass
5♡	Pass	6♠	Pass
Pass	Pass		

Opening lead: ◇ 4

I am glad that this hand was not bid to a contract of 6 ◇, which could survive even the 5-0 trump break, because it gives you, East, an opportunity to shine defensively in what may have been the greatest defensive coup I have ever witnessed.

No doubt East's double of 4 ◇ should not have fooled South as it did. East was aiming at getting a diamond ruff against the eventual club or spade contract, hoping that if South redoubled the escape to four hearts wouldn't be too severe a penalty. But when West led the ◇ 4, declarer visualized losing the diamond finesse and having the second diamond ruffed. So he put up North's ◇ A and was shocked when East trumped.

Nevertheless, as East you will have to produce some spectacular defensive maneuvers to set the contract.

Take over.

it's hard to score a one-punch knockout   81.

From the bidding, East can be sure that South has no natural trump loser. He holds the ace of hearts; he'll be able to score a heart ruff if he needs it, and the club suit is sure to furnish sufficient discards of losing diamonds. If. . . . The big "if" is that South may not have more than a single club, so that he can be cut off from dummy with an immediate club lead.

The club switch forces declarer to take diamond discards immediately, and he does so on the second and third club tricks. But he still has two losing hearts to take care of and he must get to his hand twice in order to ruff them. The safe way is by leading diamonds, for he knows that West cannot overruff. But East is now in a position to deliver two deadly uppercuts.

He ruffs the second diamond lead with the ♠ 10. South has to overruff and he trumps a heart. Next he leads another diamond from dummy and East uppercuts with the ♠ J, forcing declarer to spend another high trump to ruff his last heart loser in dummy. Now dummy leads another diamond and all would be well if East had started with four trumps and West held only a singleton.

But such is not the case. South ruffs and cashes his lone remaining high spade. But it isn't enough. West's ♠ 9 stands up to defeat the slam.

LET YOUR CONSCIOUSNESS BE YOUR GUIDE: Don't rely on such rules as "through strength up to weakness." Sometimes — and if you can count the hands out from the bidding and play you will know when — leading up to strength can be the winning defense. In this deal, even the small clue that West led the ◇ 4 and South played the ◇ 3 will help in counting South for a holding of three cards in diamonds.

Vulnerable: N-S
Dealer: S

```
                    ♠ A Q 3
                    ♡ A 10 9 8 6 3
                    ◇ J 3
                    ♣ 4 2

  ♠ J 8 6 2              N              ♠ 4
  ♡ J 5          W            E         ♡ Q 7 2
  ◇ K 5 4                              ◇ Q 9 8 6 2
  ♣ J 10 9 6            S              ♣ Q 7 5 3

                    ♠ K 10 9 7 5
                    ♡ K 4
                    ◇ A 10 7
                    ♣ A K 8
```

The bidding:

SOUTH	WEST	NORTH	EAST
1♠	Pass	2♡	Pass
2NT	Pass	4♠	Pass
6♠	Pass	Pass	Pass

Opening lead: ♣ J

North had a difficult second bid and chose to jump-raise on only three spades to the A-Q. If opener does not raise a 2♡ response, as he would surely do with three-card support, it is generally a good bet that his 1♠ bid was on a five-card suit since the chances are that, with a four-card suit and fewer than three hearts, he would have opened 1♣ or 1◇.

South won the first trick with the ♣K and saw that with reasonable breaks in both majors the slam would be easy. His challenge, and yours, is, how best to guard against an evil split.

82. how to be a successful pessimist

A good bridge player must be both an optimist and a pessimist. When you need good breaks, you must be an optimist. When you can afford to play safe, you should be a pessimist. The trick is to know when and how to be each. South planned his campaign to guard against four trumps in either hand or four hearts with East.

In similar situations concerning only the play of the trump suit, it would be correct to cash dummy's ♠AQ. Then, if West showed out, South would have a marked finesse against East's ♠J. But if played on this line, dummy would have no entry to the hearts unless the ♡QJ were unguarded; so South quickly rejected this plan. Then how could he guard against bad breaks? The answer: only by keeping two spade entries to dummy. South had found the right way to be a pessimist.

Had declarer played the ♠AK before leading

hearts, he would cash the ♡K and ♡A, then ruff the third heart. If West were foolish enough to overruff, this scheme would work. But it would fail if West simply discarded. He would still have a trump left when declarer returned to dummy's ♠Q. West would ruff the fourth heart with his good ♠J, but declarer would be able to discard only one loser and would go down two tricks.

The winning play was to cash the ♠K at the second trick, then lead ♡K, cross to the ♡A, and ruff a third heart with the ♠10. Now it wouldn't matter if West overruffed or not. A second spade lead would put dummy in to lead good hearts. Whenever West chose to ruff, the ♠A would remain in North's hand serving to draw West's last trump while putting dummy in to run the remaining hearts.

Vulnerable: N-S
Dealer: S

```
            ♠  K J 8 4
            ♡  J 7
            ◇  10 9 6 5 3
            ♣  A 10

♠  9 3              N           ♠  10 7 6 5 2
♡  10 9 8 6 4                   ♡  5 3 2
◇  K Q 7 2      W       E       ◇  4
♣  8 6              S           ♣  J 9 5 4

            ♠  A Q
            ♡  A K Q
            ◇  A J 8
            ♣  K Q 7 3 2
```

If the adversely-held East-West cards were reshuffled, and East and West were each given 13 new cards, South would fulfill his slam contract over 90% of the time no matter how he played the hand. But it would take a good player to make it almost 100% of the time.

Are you that good a player?

The bidding:

SOUTH	WEST	NORTH	EAST
3NT	Pass	6NT	Pass
Pass	Pass		

Opening lead: ♡ 10

pessimism: the essential attribute

After winning the opening lead with the ♡ K, declarer cashed the ♠ A and ♠ Q. Had a less-gifted player been occupying the South seat, he probably would next have entered dummy via the ♣ A to cash the ♠ K and ♠ J, expecting that the outstanding spades would be divided normally, 4–3. South would discard the eight and jack of diamonds. Next would come two more club leads to South's ♣ K and ♣ Q, hoping that the six missing clubs were divided no worse than 4–2, in which case South's fifth club would become his slam-going trick.

As is evident, however, East's fifth spade had become a winner. And when East obtained the lead in clubs, that spade would take the setting trick. Declarer would then probably bemoan his fate — and possibly add that if it were only West who possessed the fifth spade, the slam would be made.

At tricks two and three, our actual South did cash the ♠ A and ♠ Q. But when he next led a club, he did not play dummy's ♣ A. Instead, he "finessed" the ♣ 10. East won the trick with his ♣ J, but that was the end of the line for the defenders. When East returned a diamond, South took his ◇ A, entered dummy via the ♣ A to cash the ♠ K and ♠ J, discarding thereon his ◇ 8 and ◇ J. He then claimed his contract, winning four spades, three hearts, one diamond, and four clubs.

Only in the hardly likely event that East had been dealt the singleton ♣ J, or five including the ♣ J, would this line of play have failed.

And if *West* happened to have those five clubs, then the finesse of the ♣ 10 would have brought in four club tricks and the slam contract.

(N-S 60 part score)
Vulnerable: None
Dealer: E

```
                    ♠ J 10 7 5 4
                    ♡ 7 6
                    ◇ 9 7 2
                    ♣ 9 3 2

♠  --                              ♠ A 8 6 2
♡ J 8 4 3          N               ♡ K Q 10 9
◇ K 10 8 6 4    W     E            ◇ J 5
♣ Q J 8 7          S               ♣ K 6 4

                    ♠ K Q 9 3
                    ♡ A 5 2
                    ◇ A Q 3
                    ♣ A 10 5
```

The bidding will tell you that this hand did not occur recently, else East might have preferred another bid rather than open 1♠ on so weak a suit. But the hand did occur; it posed a problem that was solved brilliantly by none other than Howard Schenken and you are invited to equal his performance with the South hand.

South did not need the opening lead of the ◇ 6 to tell him that West didn't have a spade to lead. But he did need to find a way to harvest North's long spades. Do you have a plan?

The bidding:

EAST	SOUTH	WEST	NORTH
1♠	1NT	2◇	Pass
Pass	2NT	Pass	Pass
Pass			

Opening lead: ◇ 6

84. a famous play by a famous player

You have won the first trick with the ◇ Q and you count your tricks: Two diamonds, one club, one heart and some spades. To make your contract, you are going to need North's fifth spade. But if you lead out spades, East will have no trouble perceiving that he cannot afford to win a spade trick early, but must hold up his ♠ A until the fourth round. What to do about it?

Since you know that West does not have a spade, presumably he has led from his longest suit. If so, and if you can force East to make at least one discard, what would be more likely than that he discard the useless small spade with which he cannot hope to take a trick?

And that is exactly what happened, even though it was Sam Fry, Jr., a great star in his own right, who held the East cards.

South led a low diamond to the second trick. West grabbed this trick and was happy to lead a third diamond, establishing the suit. On this third diamond lead, won by South's ◇ A, East discarded the ♠ 2. And now he could no longer hold up the ♠ A for long enough to kill dummy's fifth card in the suit. He won the ♠ A and shifted to the ♡ K, but it was no use. Schenken took the ♡ A, cashed four tricks in the spade suit, and made his contract with the ♣ A.

Here I am glad to say something about the good sportsmanship of Sam Fry. It was Sam, not Howard, who gave this hand its great publicity by telling about it to all who would listen.

By the way, did you come up with Schenken's brilliant coup?

Vulnerable: None
Dealer: W

♠ A 10 4
♡ A Q 8 4 2
♢ K 8
♣ J 8 7

♠ K Q J 7 6 5   ♠ —
♡ J 7 6   ♡ 10 9 5 3
♢ 10 6   ♢ Q J 7 4 3
♣ 10 3   ♣ A Q 6 4

♠ 9 8 3 2
♡ K
♢ A 9 5 2
♣ K 9 5 2

The bidding:

WEST	NORTH	EAST	SOUTH
Pass	1♣	1♢	Dbl. (negative)
1♠	2♡	Pass	2NT
Pass	3NT	Pass	Pass
Pass			

Opening lead: ♠ K

One reason Benito Garozzo seems to be involved in so many spectacular hands is that he is a bold bidder. He was playing South in an infrequent partnership with Walter Avarelli, when he met this challenge in the Team Championship at the 1971 Rabat Festival.

North-South arrived at an optimistic 3NT contract after Avarelli, North, took a bit of license in using a Roman one club opening with a five-card heart suit.

West's opening lead was ducked, and East discarded the ♣ 6. West shifted to the ♢ 10, won by North's ♢ K, and Benito pushed the ♣ J through. East covered with the ♣ Q and the ♣ K won the trick. A club continuation was won by West's ♣ 10 and when West led another diamond, East played the ♢ J. How do you proceed?

Here's your chance to share the gallery's applause that followed declarer's bringing home his 3NT contract.

even an open book may need a bookmark!

Success in this deal requires counting out the opponent's distribution. The play thus far has revealed West's hand: Six spades when East showed out on the first lead; two clubs, since East is known to have the missing ♣ A; two diamonds, from West's lead of the ♢ 10 as well as from East's overcall. This leaves him exactly three hearts, and the layout, with South still to play on the ♢ J, must be:

♠ A 10
♡ A Q 8 4 2
♢ —
♣ 8

♠ Q J 7 6 5   ♠ —
♡ ? ? ?   ♡ ? ? ? ?
♢ —   ♢ Q 7 4
♣ —   ♣ A

♠ 9 8 3
♡ K
♢ A 9 5
♣ 9 5

If West holds the ♡ J109, everything is easy, but that isn't too likely. Nor is it necessary for him to have any special cards in hearts, since you know he has only three.

Habit might persuade you to duck the diamond in order to hold a tenace over East's ♢ Q7. But East would shift to a heart, knocking out your ♡ K and your reentry to the ♣ 9 you intend to establish. So you must grab the ♢ A without delay and knock out the ♣ A. If East cashes the ♢ Q, you will make three diamonds, two clubs, three hearts and one spade trick. So East can't afford to cash his high diamond. Instead, he knocks out your ♡ K. On the ♣ 9 you discard a heart from dummy, then lead toward the ♠ A10.

West must put in an honor. You win with dummy's ♠ A, cash the ♡ A Q, exhausting West of that suit, and lead dummy's ♠ 10. West cannot prevent you from winning your ninth trick in the spade suit, and you have earned a share of Garozzo's applause.

Vulnerable: Both
Dealer: N

```
                    ♠ A 6 5
                    ♡ J 7 3 2
                    ◊ K 9
                    ♣ A Q 10 6

  ♠ J 8              N          ♠ Q 10 2
  ♡ 9 4                         ♡ A K Q 10 8 5
  ◊ J 8 7 5 4     W     E       ◊ A 10 2
  ♣ 9 8 4 3          S          ♣ 2

                    ♠ K 9 7 4 3
                    ♡ 6
                    ◊ Q 6 3
                    ♣ K J 7 5
```

The bidding:

NORTH	EAST	SOUTH	WEST
1♣	2♡	2♠	Pass
3♠	Pass	4♠	Pass
Pass	Pass		

Opening lead: ♡ 9

The modern trend in overcalls has been toward weak jumps. But there are some old-fashioned virtues to the old-fashioned strong type, and many players still prefer to reserve the jump overcall to indicate a powerful one-suited hand or a strong two-suiter.

East was using the bid in this fashion, so he was marked with the ◊ A, as well as a powerful heart suit. In fact, he overtook the lead of the ♡ 9 with the ♡ 10 and continued the suit. South ruffed, West following with the ♡ 4. It must be obvious to you as declarer that West doesn't have another heart.

How do you plan your play?

86. how can you make sure?

If you could be sure that West held exactly three trumps, you wouldn't mind being overruffed when East takes his ◊ A and leads another heart. You expect to lose a trump trick anyway. But if West gets an overruff holding a doubleton trump, you must still lose a second trump trick to East.

There's a reasonable chance that West holds the spade length based on the fact that East has only seven cards outside the heart suit while West has eleven. But, while 7–11 are winning numbers in craps, your game is bridge and your challenge is to make your contract — assuming the necessary 3–2 trump break — no matter which defender has three.

The actual South who played this hand took the ♠ A and ♠ K and lost the ◊ K to East's ◊ A. East produced the ♠ Q, extracting dummy's potential ruffer, and declarer had to lose a second diamond trick. Had West held the ♠ Q instead of East, South would have been able to ruff the losing diamond with dummy's remaining trump. Yet, if you had failed to draw two rounds of trumps, when East won the ◊ A, West would get a heart overruff.

The winning plan is to play the ♠ K and ♠ A, ending in dummy, then lead a low diamond. If East rises with the ◊ A, you won't need to ruff a diamond. Your ◊ K and ◊ Q are winners. If East plays low, your ◊ Q takes the trick. You cross to dummy's ♣ 10, ruff a heart and lead a club to dummy. If East doesn't ruff, you trump dummy's last heart and continue clubs. Any time East ruffs, he can also cash the ◊ A, but a trump will remain in dummy to take care of the third diamond.

Note that your scheme depends only on East's holding the ◊ A and succeeds equally well if West holds the third trump.

Vulnerable: Both
Dealer: S

```
                 ♠  A 10 6 4 2
                 ♡  8 3 2
                 ◇  J 7 4
                 ♣  K 7
♠  J 9 8 7 3                        ♠  K Q
♡  J              N                 ♡  K 9 7 6
◇  8 6 2     W        E             ◇  9 5
♣  Q J 9 8        S                 ♣  6 5 4 3 2
                 ♠  5
                 ♡  A Q 10 5 4
                 ◇  A K Q 10 3
                 ♣  A 10
```

South was overly aggressive when he bid 4 NT to ask for aces. Even a mere 5 ♡ contract might have been in jeopardy had North held, for example:

♠ KQ10xx ♡ 9xx ◇ xxx ♣ Qx

Finding the ♠ A and ♣ K among North's values still left the slam less than a laydown. In fact, South didn't make it.

Would you have brought it home?

The bidding:

SOUTH	WEST	NORTH	EAST
1 ♡	Pass	1 ♠	Pass
3 ◇	Pass	3 ♡	Pass
4 ◇	Pass	4 ♡	Pass
4 NT	Pass	5 ◇	Pass
6 ♡	Pass	Pass	Pass

Opening lead: ♣ Q

South had to play the spots off 'em 87.

Declarer knew that in most instances where you are missing five trumps including the king and jack, the proper way to provide for the loss of only a single trick is to take two finesses. Since the finesse of the 10 might often fetch the king, it is customary to play that card first.

Therefore, South won the first trick with the ♣ K and finessed the ♡ 10, losing to the ♡ J. Since the ♣ 10 appeared on the first trick, West knew it was safe to continue clubs, forcing South's ♣ A. Declarer crossed to dummy's ♠ A and repeated the trump finesse as planned. The ♡ Q won, and although dummy still had the ◇ J as a reentry, it was of no value. South had to lose a second trump trick, and with it his small slam.

Odds-ly enough, the first-round finesse of the ♡ 10 would have been correct if South's trump holding had also included the ♡ 9. As you will see, he could then have used the ♠ A to take another finesse and pick up East's ♡ K, even though it was still guarded.

With the cards he held, however, South's play of the ♡ 10 could not prevail even if it fetched the singleton ♡ K. With East holding ♡ J976, declarer would still have to concede a second trump trick.

Look it up in *The Official Encyclopedia of Bridge,* if you like. The entry is under "Suit Combinations" and it will confirm that unless you need to run the entire suit without loss, finessing the 10 is correct only when holding the 9; without it, the proper play is to finesse the Q first. Here, if the ♡ Q wins, South should enter dummy via the ♠ A to lead toward the closed hand, planning to insert the ♡ 10 if a lower heart appears. The ◇ J remains as an additional entry to dummy if needed to cope with ♠ KJ9x in the East hand.

Vulnerable: Both
Dealer: S

```
                    ♠ A 9 7 5 3 2
                    ♡ 7 5
                    ◇ 10 5
                    ♣ A 8 2
  ♠ J 10 8 4              N          ♠ 6
  ♡ 9                                ♡ K J 8 6 3 2
  ◇ K 6 2          W        E        ◇ Q 4 3
  ♣ K 10 6 4 3            S          ♣ J 9 5
                    ♠ K Q
                    ♡ A Q 10 4
                    ◇ A J 9 8 7
                    ♣ Q 7
```

If you do not find the winning play by South in this deal, you may console yourself with the fact that few experts did, even when it was presented to them as a problem.

Which is why my great friend, Harold Ogust, deserves credit for having found the successful line in a rubber bridge game, where it involved a mere matter of money, not the winning of a national championship.

As declarer, South, you let the lead ride round to your ♣ Q; East plays the ♣ J and you win the trick. It's your move.

The bidding:

SOUTH	WEST	NORTH	EAST
1 ◇	Pass	1 ♠	Pass
2 ♡	Pass	2 ♠	Pass
2NT	Pass	3NT	Pass
Pass	Pass		

Opening lead: ♣ 4

88. a thought in time saves nine

A good insurance man is usually able to convince a prospect that a small premium is worth paying if it safeguards the contract. But South's problem was to find a premium payment that would enhance his chances of bringing home the game. Càn you?

Counting his "sure" tricks, declarer could see that if spades were breaking, he had ten readily available. Now, whenever you can count ten and you need only nine, you should look for a way to sacrifice one in order to have a better chance of bringing home the game.

If you cashed the ♠ K Q before you took this into account, you're too late to consider locking the barn door. Your horse went that-a-way. You have failed to consider that, with but a single entry to dummy, you cannot bring in the spade suit if it does not split. You will need to find some other source to bring your trick total to nine. Diamonds, for example.

If East had held the four spades, perhaps when West failed to follow to the second spade lead, you'd have made an alternate plan. Ogust didn't need that reminder. When he overtook the ♠ Q with the ♠ A, he risked losing a sixth spade trick, but he could do with only five if East followed suit, surrendering one spade but winning two clubs and two aces. When East showed out after the overtake with the ♠ A, Ogust had the lead where he needed it — in dummy.

Abandoning the spade suit, he led the ◇ 10. As long as East held either two or three diamonds to an honor, declarer was bound to win four diamond tricks, whether or not East covered the ◇ 10. With the ♣ A in dummy for another diamond lead if necessary, South had given himself the extra chance that brought home his contract.

Suppose the spades had split. Then you'll have to apologize to partner for your "error."

Vulnerable: Both
Dealer: S

```
                 ♠ A J 7
                 ♡ J 10 5 4
                 ◇ 5 4
                 ♣ Q 10 8 6

♠ 8 5 2                        ♠ K 9 4 3
♡ 8 7 2          N            ♡ K Q 9 6
◇ J 9 7 2     W     E         ◇ 10 8 6
♣ K 7 5          S            ♣ 4 2

                 ♠ Q 10 6
                 ♡ A 3
                 ◇ A K Q 3
                 ♣ A J 9 3
```

The bidding:

SOUTH	WEST	NORTH	EAST
2NT	Pass	3♣	Pass
3◇	Pass	3NT	Pass
Pass	Pass		

Opening lead: ♡ 8

Dummy covered East's opening lead of the ♡ 8 with the ♡ 10 and declarer won the queen with his ace. Declarer toyed with the idea of refusing the spade finesse in order to get to dummy quickly for a club hook, but three clubs wouldn't be enough to bring the total to nine tricks, whereas, if the club finesse worked, the contract was never in danger.

So declarer led to the ♠ J, losing to the ♠ K. A diamond shift didn't cause any embarrassment. South won with the ◇ A, crossed to dummy's ♠ A and ran the ♣ 10. Two finesses wrong out of two. West won with the ♣ K, pushed the ♡ 7 through, and the defenders had five tricks. Tough luck. But could it have been overcome?

when normal play isn't good enough   89.

Declarer was right to take the spade finesse because the heart suit could not be profitably continued from East's side of the table. If he had declined the finesse, it would not have helped. West gets in with the ♣ K and continues hearts for three tricks. Then the ♠ K provides the setting trick.

But do you see how declarer can insure his contract?

The opening lead of ♡ 8 is obviously top of nothing, but even if it isn't and the dummy's ♡ 10 would hold the first trick, South doesn't need it. He can afford to lose two hearts and the two black kings and still make his game. What he CANNOT afford is to lose three heart tricks.

The way to assure this is to play low from dummy on the opening lead and win the trick with the ace! The ♠ J finesse is lost, but East can't profitably continue hearts from his side of the table. Dummy gets in with the ♠ A for a losing club finesse, but West can't establish three heart tricks for his partner because on the next heart North's ♡ 10 is played. East must win the trick, and East can't continue hearts without yielding another stopper.

Strangely enough, South would have been saved from error if he had held a singleton heart ace. The mere fact that he began with a doubleton was no excuse for putting the contract on the floor. Declarer didn't need to win a second heart trick to make his contract. He needed only to make sure that the opponents did not win three tricks in the suit.

Vulnerable: Both
Dealer: N

```
                ♠ K 7 4 2
                ♡ 6 5 3
                ◇ A K Q J 10
                ♣ 4

    ♠ Q 8 5 3          N          ♠ 6
    ♡ K Q 10                      ♡ 9 7 4 2
    ◇ 7 5        W         E      ◇ 8 6 3 2
    ♣ A K 10 3         S          ♣ Q 8 6 5

                ♠ A J 10 9
                ♡ A J 8
                ◇ 9 4
                ♣ J 9 7 2
```

East played the ♣8 on his partner's ♣K, but West shifted to the ♡K nonetheless. South ducked and West shifted back to a low club, ruffed in dummy.

South congratulated himself that the partnership had escaped a 3NT contract which might depend on guessing the ♠Q. At 4♠, guessing who had the ♠Q seemed unnecessary. How would you play the trump suit if you were declarer?

The bidding:

NORTH	EAST	SOUTH	WEST
1◇	Pass	1♠	Pass
2♠	Pass	2NT	Pass
4♠	Pass	Pass	Pass

Opening lead: ♣K

90. nothing succeeds like failure

The most convenient way to play the trumps was to take an immediate finesse to the ♠9, which held the trick. So declarer crossed to the ♠K, planning to repeat the finesse against East if necessary — but East showed out!

Declarer saved what he could from the wreckage. He crossed to the ♡A and trumped another club with dummy's last spade. Then he led diamonds, hoping that West would have to follow to at least three leads of the suit. But when South discarded his last club West ruffed the third diamond. South had been able to shed only one of his two remaining losers. Down one!

The hand is reminiscent of the tale of the declarer who successfully finessed for a queen against one opponent, then finessed for it against the other. To his partner's "Why?" he said, "It worked so well the first time, I thought I'd try it the other way."

Idiotic though this may sound, it was the only correct way to play this hand. Once both opponents had followed to the first trump lead, taking the finesse the other way would insure the contract against any distribution except a void in diamonds in West's hand and a doubleton ♠Q with East. Surely this was more remote than that West had been guileful enough to refuse to take his ♠Q on the first trump lead.

Give West all due credit for having made a beautiful play. But, even if declarer knew that the actual West would never have been capable of making such a splendid play intentionally, there was always the chance that he might have pulled the wrong card by mistake. You cannot often allow yourself the luxury of guarding against this happenstance, but this deal was one of those rare occasions when you could. And should!

Vulnerable: N-S
Dealer: S

```
                ♠  8 6 2
                ♡  4 3 2
                ◇  K Q 5 4
                ♣  A Q 5
♠  J 10 9                        ♠  A K 7 3
♡  –              N              ♡  K J 9 8 6
◇  9 6 3      W       E          ◇  J 10 2
♣  K J 9 8 6 3 2     S           ♣  7
                ♠  Q 5 4
                ♡  A Q 10 7 5
                ◇  A 8 7
                ♣  10 4
```

The bidding:

SOUTH	WEST	NORTH	EAST
1♡	3♣	3NT	Dbl.
Pass	Pass	4♡	Dbl.
Pass	Pass	Pass	

Opening lead: ♠ J

Even when they are as weak as West's 3♣ bid, weak jump overcalls seem to bear a charmed life, so North preferred to try for a vulnerable game at notrump. East didn't believe the opponents could make 3NT, but was really delighted when his double drove them from a nine-trick game that could have been made to a ten-trick game that "obviously" couldn't.

The defenders started off collecting their two top spades and South won the third round of the suit. The ◇ Q furnished entry for a heart lead and East put in the ♡ 8, fearful that if he did not South would have finessed the ♡ 7, as indeed he might have. South finessed the ♡ 10 and was not really surprised at the sight of West's club discard. The ◇ A was cashed and the ♣ Q finessed for a repeated heart lead. East played the ♡ 9 to force South's ♡ Q. Do you see any way for South to make his contract?

want a handicap? OK, you may peek   91.

The declarer's problem was virtually a double dummy one, so you may study the position as declarer went back to dummy with the ◇ K and led the thirteenth diamond.

```
                ♠  —
                ♡  4
                ◇  4
                ♣  A 5
♠  —                         ♠  7
♡  —                         ♡  K J 6
◇  —                         ◇  —
♣  K J 9 8                   ♣  —
                ♠  —
                ♡  A 7 5
                ◇  —
                ♣  10
```

Obviously East couldn't afford to discard his ♠ 7. Neither could he successfully ruff with the ♡ 6. South would overruff with the ♡ 7, cash the ♡ A and lead to the ♣ A, forcing out East's last trump and so losing only one trump trick. So East ruffed with the ♡ J. If South discarded, he'd have to win a spade return and concede a trump trick to East's ♡ K. If, instead, South overruffed with the ♡ A, the lead would be in his hand and East would have two natural trump tricks.

But declarer found a solution. He underruffed, "discarding" the ♡ 5. East was hooked. If he led a trump, declarer would cash the ♡ A 7 and score the last trick with the ♣ A. If East led a spade, South would discard his ♣ 10 and ruff in dummy. With the lead coming through East, South's ♡ A 7 would score the last two trump tricks.

Vulnerable: Both
Dealer: S

```
                    ♠  A 6
                    ♡  Q 10 9 4
                    ◇  —
                    ♣  A K J 6 5 4 3
♠  K 7 5                              ♠  9 8 4 2
♡  8 7 5 3          N                 ♡  2
◇  J 10 9 7 2    W     E              ◇  A 8 5 3
♣  7                S                 ♣  Q 10 9 8
                    ♠  Q J 10 3
                    ♡  A K J 6
                    ◇  K Q 6 4
                    ♣  2
```

North's cue-bid in diamonds was a way of fishing for a club preference, but when South raised diamonds it became obvious that the contract belonged in hearts.

As South, you have to prepare to overcome some bad breaks. The principal menace is that if dummy ruffs diamonds and South has to ruff clubs to set up that suit, a bad trump break will beat you.

From here on, you're on your own.

The bidding:

SOUTH	WEST	NORTH	EAST
1 ♠	Pass	3 ♣	Pass
3 ♡	Pass	4 ◇	Pass
5 ◇	Pass	6 ♡	Pass
Pass	Pass		

Opening lead: ◇ J

92. giving an ace an intentional pass

Having decided to protect dummy's trump length, you adopt a "loser on loser" line that safeguards your contract. Or does it?

Not if you elected to dump dummy's spade loser on the first trick. Back comes a spade to the ♠ A. You cash the ♣ A and ruff a low club with a high trump. West shows out and you need to ruff another club to set up the suit. So you lead to the ♡ 9, trump another club with the ♡ A and cash the ♡ J. All would be well if the trumps divided. You could win the rest of the tricks without even cashing a high diamond. Simply ruff a diamond or a spade, draw the last trump and run the good clubs. But West has begun with four trumps and you cannot get to dummy without ruffing something. So even if you cash the ◇ KQ, you wind up short.

What was your rush to discard the losing spade?

Once the ◇ A was gone, there was plenty of time to discard a spade on your ◇ K. Meanwhile, it was highly important to save the guard for dummy's ♠ A.

Note what happens if East shifts to spades while dummy still has a low one. If West doesn't cover your ♠ Q with the ♠ K, you have preserved the ♠ A as an essential entry without needing to ruff anything in dummy. If West covers the ♠ Q with the ♠ K to force dummy's ♠ A, you change your plan and set up your own hand rather than dummy. The play goes ♠ A, ♡ 10, ♡ A, diamond ruff. Now you get back to your hand by leading dummy's last trump. Draw West's remaining trumps, cash the ◇ KQ and the ♠ 10 and get rid of your only remaining loser — the low spade — by crossing to dummy's ♣ A K.

The moral: Before playing loser-on-loser, make sure you are actually discarding a loser.

Vulnerable: Both
Dealer: N

♠ A K 4 3
♡ 6 5
◇ A K Q 3
♣ K 5 4

♠ Q 10 6
♡ K J 8 7
◇ J 8
♣ Q J 8 6

N
W   E
S

♠ 9 8 7 2
♡ A 3
◇ 10 9 6 2
♣ 7 3 2

♠ J 5
♡ Q 10 9 4 2
◇ 7 5 4
♣ A 10 9

The bidding:

NORTH	EAST	SOUTH	WEST
1◇	Pass	1♡	Pass
1♠	Pass	1NT	Pass
3NT	Pass	Pass	Pass

Opening lead: ♡ 7

This puzzler is so rare that for once you are allowed to remove your thumbs from the defender's cards and play as if you could see them.

It's fairly obvious how you came to be in 3NT with the South cards. West decided that your Achilles heel might be the suit you had bid, and his heart opening was won by the ♡ A. You dropped the ♡ 4, hoping to foster the idea that you had started with only a four-card suit, and you played the ♡ 9 on the second trick, forcing West's ♡ J. But West saw no future in continuing the suit and shifted to the ♣ Q, presenting you with all kinds of chances to make your contract. But do you see the one sure-fire way?

you can't trump your partner's trick at notrump   93.

If you have examined your plentiful chances, you can see that by winning the ♣ A and pushing the ♣ 10 through West's ♣ J, you have three sure club tricks. Now, assuming that West doesn't cover the ♣ 10, you lead a diamond to dummy and play a low spade toward your ♠ J. If East has the ♠ Q, you are due to make nine tricks. If not, you still have the possibility of a diamond split.

But if you played it that way without looking at the opponents' cards, you'd be the victim of extreme hard luck. And if you played it that way seeing where all the cards are, you'd be the victim of only a slight touch of myopia. Yes, dear reader, there is a *sure* way to make your contract. Care to try again?

The answer is to swap one trick for two. By giving up

a trick, you gain an extra reentry. How? Cover West's ♣ Q with North's ♣ K and overtake it with your ♣ A! Now lead a heart to force out West's ♡ K. West will be given another club trick, but that is only his side's fourth trick and no matter how he defends he cannot establish enough defensive tricks, nor can he prevent you from gaining the lead in clubs and cashing two good hearts.

Add them up. You score two hearts, two clubs, two spades and three diamonds. Giving up a trick in time — perhaps we might say giving up a trick *to* time — saves nine.

As we truly observed, you can't trump your partner's trick at notrump. But you can overtake it, and this is one time when you should.

Vulnerable: E-W
Dealer: S

♠	A J 10 9
♡	10 8 7 5
◇	A Q J 8
♣	4

West	East
♠ Q 8 6 5 3 2	♠ K
♡ —	♡ A 9 6 3
◇ 9 7 6 4 2	◇ 3
♣ 7 3	♣ K Q J 10 9 8 6

N
W E
S

♠	7 4
♡	K Q J 4 2
◇	K 10 5
♣	A 5 2

South's problem didn't come until late in the play of this deal. He won the club lead with the ♣ A and ruffed a club. Next he led a heart from dummy to his ♡ J and West showed out. On the third club lead West showed out again. Dummy ruffed and led the ♡ 10. Once again East ducked and South could not afford to overtake without conceding two heart tricks to East's ♡ A-9.

It's up to you to get back and forth without losing two trump tricks.

The bidding:

SOUTH	WEST	NORTH	EAST
1 ♡	Pass	1 ♠	4 ♣
Pass	Pass	4 ◇	Pass
4 ♡	Pass	5 ♡	Pass
6 ♡	Pass	Pass	Pass

Opening lead: ♣ 7

94. lock the doors before you lose your horse

You have a count on eleven of East's thirteen cards. He has turned up with seven clubs and four hearts. There are only two cards in his hand that you do not know. What are they?

Obviously, unless one of them is a diamond, you won't be able to get to your hand without East ruffing with the ♡ 9 and scoring the ♡ A. So you lead to the ◇ 10 and play the ♡ K, but you haven't thought things out sufficiently. East takes the ♡ A and returns the ♠ K, leaving you in dummy and knowing that East will ruff whatever card you lead.

You see now that you should have barred the exit door. But how could you have known whether East had a spade or another diamond?

As it so often does, the answer lies in going back to the bidding. You were forced to play for East to have **at least one diamond**, or you couldn't get back to your hand.

Purely on the number of cards outstanding in each suit, you might have guessed that his other card was a spade. But there was a much more reliable clue.

With a void in spades and the ace of trumps, surely East would have doubled your slam bid, asking partner for an unusual lead. It wouldn't be hard for West to figure what was called for; most often, it is a lead in dummy's first bid suit and in this case, if West held seven spades, the lead East wanted would be a sure thing. But East had *not* doubled, so he must have a spade in his hand.

The winning play is now clear. You should have cashed dummy's ♠ A before you came off dummy with a diamond. Then, on winning the ♡ A, East couldn't play anything but a club or a heart. You would be able to ruff the club, draw his last trump and discard your losing spade on dummy's fourth diamond as planned.

Vulnerable: Both
Dealer: E

```
                  ♠ K Q J
                  ♡ A K 8 3
                  ◇ K 5
                  ♣ A Q 3 2
♠ 10 8 6 3                      ♠ 5
♡ Q 10 9 6 5 2      N           ♡ 7
◇ A Q          W       E        ◇ J 9 8 7 4 2
♣ K                S            ♣ J 10 8 7 5
                  ♠ A 9 7 4 2
                  ♡ J 4
                  ◇ 10 6 3
                  ♣ 9 6 4
```

Once in a blue moon a hand comes along that is virtually a double-dummy problem—one where the solution is extremely difficult to find even though you know the exact location of the cards.

This is such a hand. West's opening third-hand weak 2 ♡ bid, his lead of an obviously singleton ♣K, and the ensuing automatic plays, ♣A, ♠K and ♠Q, with East discarding the ◇2 on the second spade lead, give South a blueprint of the hand. Yet you will find it a challenge to make your contract. See for yourself.

The bidding:

EAST	SOUTH	WEST	NORTH
Pass	Pass	2 ♡	Dbl.
Pass	2 ♠	Pass	3 ♡
Pass	4 ♠	Pass	Pass
Pass			

Opening lead: ♣ K

only one way, but it's hard to find

South wasn't quite strong enough to do more than bid 2 ♠ in response to partner's takeout double of the opening weak 2 ♡ bid, but when North cue-bid in hearts at his second turn, South showed the difference between a four-to-the-oomph forced response and his actual holding of five spades including the ♠ A.

Everything about the deal became plain after the first three tricks—everything, that is, except the only way to bring home the game. When dummy won the ♣ A and cashed the ♠ K Q, with East following only once and then discarding a low diamond, if you were the declarer, you knew that West had started with six hearts, four spades, a singleton ♣ K and presumably the ◇ A and another.

When you cash dummy's ♠ J, you can't afford to over-take it in order to draw trumps, so it seems your path must be to cash the ♡ A K, ruff a third heart and draw West's last trump with the ♠ A. Unfortunately, this also draws your last trump. You can score dummy's ♣ Q as your ninth trick, but as soon as you lead a diamond West can

grab his ◇ A and you will never get the tenth trick you need for your contract. (West can't be safely thrown in with dummy's last heart since he will discard his ◇ Q on the club lead to dummy.)

Then how can you arrange to bring home the ◇ K and your game? Take your time and see if you come up with the only answer.

The solution is to retain a heart stopper after you have drawn trumps. And the way to do that is to cash only one high heart, then lead to your ♡ J and West's ♡ Q. West continues hearts, but you hold out dummy's ♡ K, and ruff this third round of hearts with the ♠ 9—just as you did if you followed your original path, but with the big difference that you still retain heart control.

Now, when you cash the ♠ A and draw West's last trump, you lead up to dummy's ◇ K. You hold the ♡ K in dummy to prevent West from running tricks in that suit, and no matter how he plays, West cannot prevent you from collecting your precious tenth trick.

Vulnerable: E-W
Dealer: W

```
                    ♠ A Q 3
                    ♡ A K 8 5 4
                    ◊ K 9 8 7
                    ♣ J

♠ K J 8 7 5         N           ♠ 6
♡ Q J 10 9      W       E       ♡ 7 3
◊ 6 2               S           ◊ 5 3
♣ A Q                           ♣ 10 8 7 6 5 4 3 2

                    ♠ 10 9 4 2
                    ♡ 6 2
                    ◊ A Q J 10 4
                    ♣ K 9
```

North bid somewhat aggressively to get to a slam. But the contract would have been virtually a laydown if West had opened the ♣ A, a card he was marked with for his opening bid.

However, West's actual lead was the ♡ Q. How should South play his slam?

The bidding:

WEST	NORTH	EAST	SOUTH
1♠	Dbl.	2♣	3◊
Pass	3♡	Pass	3NT
Pass	4♠	Pass	5◊
Pass	6◊	Pass	Pass
Pass			

Opening lead: ♡ Q

96. a case of forced hara-kiri

Although the opening lead suggested otherwise, there was a chance that a heart ruff might set up two club discards. But after the ♡ A and ♡ K won the first tricks, East showed out on the third heart. To increase his entries to dummy, South ruffed with the ◊ Q, overtook the ◊ J with North's ◊ K and ruffed a fourth heart with the ◊ A. The ◊ 4 put dummy in and, when trumps broke, South was ready to take a discard on the fifth heart in this position:

```
                ♠ A Q 3
                ♡ 8
                ◊ 9 8
                ♣ J
♠ K J 8 7 5             ♠ 6
♡ —                     ♡ —
◊ —                     ◊ —
♣ A Q                   ♣ 10 8 7 6 5 4
                ♠ 10 9 4 2
                ♡ —
                ◊ J
                ♣ K 9
```

There was no way for declarer to avoid losing at least one club, and no way to attack the spade suit so as to avoid a spade loser. What could declarer do?

The crux of the situation was South's discard. He chose the ♣ 9, and when he led to the ♣ K and West won with the ♣ A he was hooked.

If West returned the ♣ Q, North would discard a spade while South ruffed — after which a simple spade finesse would land the slam.

If, instead of the ♣ Q, West chose to play spades, no choice could prevail. A low lead would run to South's ♠ 9. Alternatively, either spade honor would be won as cheaply as possible in dummy and South would return to his hand with the high trump to push the ♠ 10 through West's remaining honor.

South could not have made three spade tricks by leading the suit himself — but by forcing West to break the suit, declarer assured himself of no spade loser.

Vulnerable: Both
Dealer: S

```
            ♠ J 10 9 8
            ♡ K 6
            ◇ A Q 7
            ♣ 7 5 4 2
♠ K Q 6 3              ♠ A 7 4 2
♡ Q 10 8 5 4 2   N    ♡ J 7
◇ 8 6 5        W   E   ◇ K 9 3
♣ —              S    ♣ J 10 8 6
            ♠ 5
            ♡ A 9 3
            ◇ J 10 4 2
            ♣ A K Q 9 3
```

When declarer is apparently able to count nine tricks at his game contract in notrump, the tendency is to let routine take over and make the customary play dictated by good technique.

You would be wise to shake yourself up in this situation. Spend the time you might ordinarily need to devote to finding a play for your contract to uncovering, instead, some way that it might be defeated. Which should be a generous warning here.

The bidding:

SOUTH	WEST	NORTH	EAST
1♣	Pass	1♠	Pass
1NT	Pass	3♣	Pass
3NT	Pass	Pass	Pass

Opening lead: ♡ 5

dear Abby: my problem is, "What's my problem?" 97.

When a long suit is led against declarer's notrump contract, it is customary to duck when you can afford to, or to win the first trick in the hand that cannot duck later. Thus, declarer can't afford to pass a heart trick for fear that the diamond finesse will lose, giving the defenders five tricks on top. Habit would dictate winning the first trick with the ♡ K. In this case, the "good" habit would be fatal. Not being clairvoyant, South leads to his ♣ A and gets the bad news.

All would still be well if dummy had two entries in diamonds. South leads the ◇ J, but East is too smart to win this trick. He waits until the finesse is repeated, capturing the ◇ Q with his ◇ K. Dummy's ◇ A provides only one entry — not enough to pick up East's clubs, and you wind up one trick shy.

While happily counting up to nine almost certain tricks and possibly eleven if the diamonds behave kindly,

South should ask himself what might happen to wreck his rosy dream and how can he prevent it. What might happen is a terrible break in clubs and finding the ◇ K wrong. If West has four clubs, South will need a blessed event in diamonds. If East has the four clubs, however, the bad break is overcome provided declarer makes sure of two reentries to dummy.

How? Win the first trick with the ♡ A. Cash the ♣ A and get the bad news before it is too late. Next take the diamond finesse without worrying over whether it loses. East wins the ◇ Q with the ◇ K, and knocks out dummy's ♡ K. It doesn't matter. With the ♣ K Q 9 poised behind East's ♣ J 10 8, two leads through are enough to prevent a club loser. Instead of being set a trick, declarer actually makes five clubs, three diamonds and two hearts, bringing home an overtrick.

Vulnerable: None ♠ A 6
Dealer: W ♡ 10 3 2
◇ 8 7 4 3
♣ J 10 5 3

♠ J 8 4 3   ♠ K 10 9
♡ 5   N   ♡ J 9 6
◇ A K 5 2   W   E   ◇ J 10 9 6
♣ A 9 6 4   S   ♣ Q 7 2

♠ Q 7 5 2
♡ A K Q 8 7 4
◇ Q
♣ K 8

The bidding:

WEST	NORTH	EAST	SOUTH
1 ◇	Pass	2 ◇	4 ♡
Pass	Pass	Pass	

Opening lead: ◇ K

Knowing what bidding system your opponents follow can be just as important in the play as during the auction. If you are playing as declarer, you can often get almost as much information from what they didn't bid as from what they did.

Here, for example, is a deal that helped Alan Sontag and Peter Weichsel win the rich Cavendish Club Sweepstakes against a powerful international field. Sontag was the only declarer to make four hearts because he drew the essential inference from the fact that the opponents did not open four-card majors. Even with this broad hint, you can congratulate yourself if you are able to match the brilliance of his technique.

98. the dog that did not bark

Most declarers ruffed the second diamond lead, crossed to dummy's ♠ A and led a low spade. East took the ♠ K and continued diamonds. This caused the declarer no immediate difficulty. He trumped the diamond, ruffed a spade in dummy and ran the ♣ J, fetching the ♣ A. It appeared that South was going to make his contract since his hand was now solid.

Unfortunately, West had a fourth spade to lead and East was able to ruff with the ♡ J for the setting trick. Do you see how Sontag made his contract? And why?

The situation paralleled the famous Sherlock Holmes case, solved when the great detective asked himself why the dog had not barked in the night.

Remember that East-West were playing five-card major suit openings. If East had started with four spades, his response to his partner's opening bid would have been

1 ♠, not 2 ◇. Yet the only chance to make the contract was if East's hand included the ♠ K and ♣ Q. So, looking far ahead to what actually took place at the other tables, Sontag simply played to ruff out the ♠ K instead of playing through it.

After ruffing the diamond lead at the second trick, Sontag immediately ducked a spade. He ruffed the diamond continuation, and played one high heart. Next he went to dummy's ♠ A and successfully finessed against East's ♣ Q. West won with the ♣ A, but could not give his partner a fourth-round spade ruff because the third round had not yet been played. Instead, Sontag trumped the diamond continuation and led a low spade, with dummy ruffing out East's ♠ K. After trumps were drawn the ♠ Q produced Sontag's tenth trick.

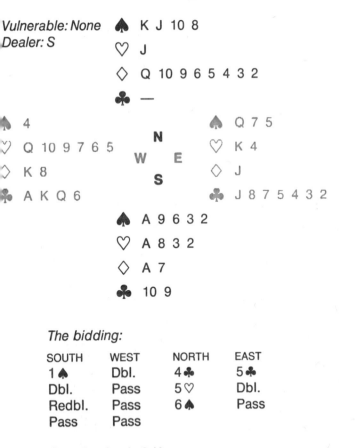

Vulnerable: None
Dealer: S

North: ♠ K J 10 8 ♡ J ♢ Q 10 9 6 5 4 3 2 ♣ —

West: ♠ 4 ♡ Q 10 9 7 6 5 ♢ K 8 ♣ A K Q 6

East: ♠ Q 7 5 ♡ K 4 ♢ J ♣ J 8 7 5 4 3 2

South: ♠ A 9 6 3 2 ♡ A 8 3 2 ♢ A 7 ♣ 10 9

The bidding:

SOUTH	WEST	NORTH	EAST
1 ♠	Dbl.	4 ♣	5 ♣
Dbl.	Pass	5 ♡	Dbl.
Redbl.	Pass	6 ♠	Pass
Pass	Pass		

Opening lead: ♣ K

We don't expect you to understand, to match, or even to envy the bidding that got Benito Garozzo to a slam in spades in this deal. Indeed, glancing at all the cards, it would seem best to play a contract of 6 ♢ — an eight-card suit that Giorgio Belladonna didn't even mention. But that would have resulted in an unremarkable slam bid, instead of winning for Benito the Charles Solomon Award for the best played hand of 1974.

Benito found himself forced to ruff the opening club lead in dummy and he had to find the ♠ Q and somehow bring home the diamonds. Ruff the first club and the opportunity to tie Benito for the Solomon award is all yours.

your chance to share the "hand of the year" award　99.

Garozzo's problem was how to establish the diamond suit and retain a reentry to cash dummy's diamond winners after trumps were drawn. There would be little difficulty in accomplishing this if the trumps were divided 2–2. But there was a strong hint, from his takeout double, that West would be short in spades. So Benito had to take steps to prepare for the likely 3–1 trump division.

Of course, there was always a chance that the ◊ K might drop singleton, but that was not to be expected. There was also the possibility that West might have the ♠ Q alone. But if the trumps were 3–1, the odds were against this and Garozzo could not afford the luxury of cashing the ♠ K to make certain. So he led the ♠ J at the second trick and let it ride. When it won, he abandoned trumps, led to ◊ A and gave up a trick to the ◊ K.

West returned another high club, shortening dummy down to one less trump than East. But it didn't matter because this was the position:

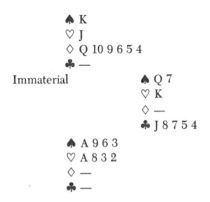

North: ♠ K ♡ J ♢ Q 10 9 6 5 4 ♣ —

Immaterial

East: ♠ Q 7 ♡ K ◊ — ♣ J 8 7 5 4

South: ♠ A 9 6 3 ♡ A 8 3 2 ◊ — ♣ —

Garozzo simply ran good diamonds from the North hand. Whenever East chose to ruff, declarer would overruff, return to dummy with the ♠ K and have more than enough good diamonds to make his slam.

Did you make the slam? We'll try to persuade Benito to lend you the plaque presented by the International Bridge Press Association for at least six months.

Vulnerable: N-S
Dealer: E

	♠ Q J 8
	♡ A J 9 6 5
	◇ K 8 2
	♣ A Q

♠ 7 6 5	**N**	♠ 4 3 2
♡ K 4 3 2	**W E**	♡ Q 10 8 7
◇ J 6 5 4 3	**S**	◇ Q 10
♣ K		♣ 10 7 5 4

	♠ A K 10 9
	♡ —
	◇ A 9 7
	♣ J 9 8 6 3 2

This deal was "a might have been," played in the World Team Championship for the Bermuda Bowl. South's redouble of 5♡, showing a void, convinced North that his partner held six clubs and he assumed these included ♣K. It wasn't so, but when South played a low heart from dummy, ruffed the opening lead and played a club, the missing ♣K appeared in the right place. Now . . . play on.

The bidding:

EAST	SOUTH	WEST	NORTH
Pass	2♣	Pass	2◇
Pass	2♠	Pass	3♡
Pass	3NT	Pass	4♣
Pass	4◇	Pass	4NT
Pass	5◇	Pass	5♡
Dbl.	Redbl.	Pass	5♠
Pass	5NT	Pass	7♣
Pass	Pass	Pass	

Opening lead: ♡ 2

100. would you have won the world championship?

Your problem is to time the play so that East will be unable to win a trick even though he still holds three clubs including the ♣10. The solution is to find East with no fewer than three spades and two diamonds.

After winning dummy's ♣A you discard a diamond on the ♡A and trump a heart. Next you cash three rounds of spades and two high diamonds, ending in dummy. You trump another heart and you have achieved the crucial position.

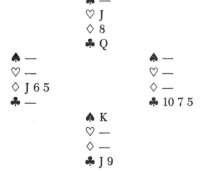

Having carefully saved dummy's ♣Q, you use it to trump your ♠K. East must underruff and when you lead a red card from dummy at trick twelve, your ♣J9 are poised to pick up his guarded ♣10.

Congratulations. But I am sorry to tell you that you are not Champion of the World; West is. You see, he actually held:

♠ 7 6 5 2   ♡ K 4 3 2   ◇ J 5 3   ♣ K 10

When he saw his ♣K trapped in front of dummy's ♣AQ he made a desperation play of the ♣K on the first trump lead — knowing that Giorgio Belladonna would find the play to pick up East's presumed ♣10xxx. East actually held only two spades; his third round spade ruff defeated your grand slam.

(P.S. It didn't actually happen. Shell-shocked at finding his ♣K in the wrong place, West neglected to play it on the first club lead.)